To Jon Davis ✓ W9-BZU-966 , '08

Enjoy the Book.

Best Wishes

The
Original Mr. Met
Remembers

Dan Reilly

"The Original Mr. Met"

The Original Mr. Met Remembers

When the Miracle Began

Dan Reilly
with Bill Curreri

iUniverse, Inc.
New York Lincoln Shanghai

The Original Mr. Met Remembers
When the Miracle Began

iUniverse books may be ordered through booksellers or by contacting:

iUniverse
2021 Pine Lake Road, Suite 100
Lincoln, NE 68512
www.iuniverse.com
1-800-Authors (1-800-288-4677)

Because of the dynamic nature of the Internet, any Web addresses or links contained in this book may have changed since publication and may no longer be valid.

The views expressed in this work are solely those of the author and do not necessarily reflect the views of the publisher, the New York Mets, or Major League Baseball, and these entities hereby disclaim any responsibility for them.

ISBN: 978-0-595-46260-5 (pbk)
ISBN: 978-0-595-70082-0 (cloth)
ISBN: 978-0-595-90560-7 (ebk)

Printed in the United States of America

Contents

Introduction

Let me introduce myself. My name is Dan Reilly. I was the original Mr. Met, the first team mascot in major league baseball history. Today baseball fans everywhere know about the Phillie Phanatic and the San Diego Chicken. The Kansas City Royals have their Sluggerrr and the Cardinals have their FredBird. All of them are descended from the original Mr. Met, who made his debut in 1964.

Mr. Met was the idea of Jim Thomson, the New York Mets' business manager, and Tom Meany, its publicity and promotion director. The Mr. Met costume was based on a cartoon character that the organization had developed for use on its tickets and promotional materials. The Mr. Met mascot brought the cartoon character to life.

I was a wide-eyed young employee in the ticket department when Jim and Tom pulled me from the ranks to be the team's mascot. I was as thrilled as a rookie being called up to the major leagues. I still remember that day in May 1964 when I first put on a Mets uniform and the Mr. Met head—made of papier-mâché and shaped like a huge baseball—and roamed the stands at Shea Stadium. Kids loved me and wanted to touch my baseball head or have their picture taken with me. I didn't realize it then, but I was making history by starting a mascot craze that would sweep through professional baseball.

Mr. Met was a sedate figure by today's standards. I was given specific instructions from management: I was to greet fans, particularly the young ones, and wave to them cheerfully—nothing more. But it was a new idea, and it opened the door for the merry escapades of today's mascots, who provide nearly as much entertainment between innings as the ballplayers do on the field.

Mr. Met fit perfectly with the personality of the Mets organization, which was innovative, offbeat, and family oriented. The early Mets players were a colorful group. They were lovable losers who made every conceivable mistake at bat, on the base paths, and in the field—yet suddenly and improbably they emerged from years of bumbling to capture the World Series in 1969. In the year of that unexpected championship, the "amazing" Mets became known as the "miracle" Mets.

This book tells the story of my adventures as Mr. Met and offers an insider's view of the players and Mets organization in the team's early years. I hope you will enjoy reading it, and I especially hope you will take pleasure in its humor.

I would like to thank several friends and loved ones who encouraged me to write this book and helped with ideas and practical assistance. My late wife, Marion, was my dearest friend and biggest fan. For years, she pushed me gently but persistently to write the book she knew I had within me. Sadly, she did not live to see the result. This book is dedicated to her memory.

Bill Curreri helped with the writing and editing and has been a joy to work with. Bob Mandt, my first boss when I joined the Mets organization, encouraged my efforts and helped provide information and facts. Bob spent forty-one years with the Mets and became vice president for baseball operations. He retired in 2004 and remains a good friend. Dick Collins, the Mets' first official photographer, has been extremely gracious in providing many photos for the book. William Medina, a colleague of mine at New York Waterway, and Dick Blodgett, a friend and neighbor, helped with many technical aspects in assembling the material and preparing it for publication. I thank them both. My friend Loretta Caputo kept me on track whenever I wavered in getting the book done. This book will be a happy surprise for her. Although she encouraged me to finish it, I didn't tell her when I completed the text and sent it to the printer. Surprise, Loretta! The first copy is for you. I wish also to thank all my friends and colleagues from the Mets and New York Waterway for their support and encouragement.

Dan Reilly
New York
July 2007

Chapter One
Looking Back

It was the twenty-fifth anniversary of the 1969 "Miracle Mets." And the entire gang—Seaver, Koosman, Swoboda, and Yogi—was there, helping to plan the festivities. Not only New York City, but the entire sports world, will never forget the thrills these young men had given us all some twenty-five summers earlier, when the improbable became reality. Just think of it. The Mets were only seven years old when they won the 1969 World Series against the heavily favored Baltimore Orioles. And while the 1997 Florida Marlins may have won a World Championship in only four years, the Mets achieved that lofty plateau in seven years without the benefit of free agency.

When the commemorative festivities were over, we all got together for a farewell lunch. Al Weis, a diminutive infielder who came through for us so many times with key hits and plays during the 1969 season, including an improbable home run in Game Five of the World Series, got up from the table and began getting autographs from all the guys. Seeing me smile, he turned to me and said, "When are we ever going to get this entire group together again?"

Al was right. This was perhaps a once-in-a-lifetime opportunity. Each year when the Mets would run the Old-Timers' Day promotion, there were usually several no-shows. Some couldn't attend for personal reasons; others, like our beloved manager and ex–Brooklyn Dodger first baseman, Gil Hodges, and the coach of that historic pitching staff, Rube Walker, were no longer with us. I decided I wasn't going to miss this opportunity, so I followed Al and made the rounds collecting autographs. Believe me, by the end of the afternoon, I wasn't alone.

Looking back to the beginning of the New York Mets franchise in the early 1960s, my first thought is not of the old Polo Grounds—the Mets' first home and the home of the New York Giants—but rather of the Martinique Hotel in New York City. It was at the Martinique that the Mets were introduced to New York City and the rest of the baseball world.

One of my old friends from the original Mets' front office, Cliff Cobb, once told me that he was the eighth employee hired by the Mets organization in 1961. They hadn't even moved into the old Polo Grounds yet. In addition to an executive office in midtown Manhattan, the Mets set up a small office at the Martinique Hotel for their sales force. Cliff, who is now a very successful Broadway ticket manager, had the unenviable task of soliciting potential season ticket buyers by telephone. He would use the Yellow Pages and start calling companies, saying, "Hello, I'm Cliff Cobb of the New York Mets. We just hired Casey Stengel as our manager and we would like to know if you would be interested in purchasing season tickets for our first season in 1962." Most of the people he contacted had never even heard of the New York Mets, and the organization hadn't even drafted its first ballplayer.

MAGIC MEMORY SERIES

The 1962 Mets were popular despite losing 120 games,
more than any other team in major league history.

While Cliff was busy trying to sell tickets for a team that hadn't even signed a player yet, the Polo Grounds stood relatively dormant. Except for a few boxing matches and some stock car races, the old ballpark hadn't really been used much since the Giants had departed for San Francisco. After the Giants and Dodgers left New York City for California in 1958, Ebbets Field, former home of the Brooklyn Dodgers, was torn down and replaced by apartment buildings. The Polo Grounds, however, remained standing. The ballpark was located atop Coogan's Bluff in the Bronx, directly across from Yankee Stadium. The two legendary ballparks were separated geographically by the Harlem River. There were certain sections in the Polo Grounds stands where you could actually see Yankee Stadium, where the hated Yankees had dominated the baseball world for decades.

Looking across the river at that mythical shrine, where Ruth, Gehrig, DiMaggio, and company had created many a baseball legend, imagine the frustration that Mets fans would experience in 1962 as their club became the most losing in baseball history. And yet the Mets went on to capture the hearts of baseball fans, both in New York

City and ultimately around the country. Since the late 1920s, the New York Yankees had developed the image of a conservative organization that was a perennial winning machine. The Mets, on the other hand, were perennial losers. Day after day they seemed to find a way to lose and break your heart. Why, then, were they so loveable? I think the average joe living in Queens or Brooklyn could easily relate to them, because he too experienced daily frustrations in his own blue-collar life.

A fatalistic attitude developed among Mets fans in those early years. This is best illustrated by a game the Mets played against the Cubs, which they actually won, 23 to 22. As the story goes, a fan who obviously enjoyed a good wager now and then asked a friend how many runs the Mets had scored that day. When told 23, he immediately asked, with a straight face, "Did they win?"

The Mets were so inept that people used to say lovingly that we would put a man on the moon before the Mets ever won a pennant. And that's exactly what happened. Neil Armstrong walked on the moon July 20, 1969. Two months later, on September 24, 1969, the Mets were National League Champions on their way to victory over the heavily favored Baltimore Orioles in the World Series. As Casey Stengel would say, "You could look it up!"

The organization's mishaps were not limited to the playing field. There is a famous story about a telephone operator who was working the switchboard at the Polo Grounds one rainy day in 1962. A game was scheduled for that afternoon, and the phones were ringing off the hook with fans inquiring about the status of the game. There were two phone numbers to call back then. If you called the general information number, you'd hear a recording that stated whether the game would be played along with general ticket information. But if you called the administration number, you could speak with a live operator. The general information number was so busy that day that one determined caller decided to dial the administration number. After the operator answered the phone with her usual, "Good afternoon, New York Mets," the caller quickly asked, "Is this a recording?" The harried operator frantically replied, "Yes, it is," and hung up the phone.

All of this frustration among Mets fans eventually needed an outlet. Fans began to bring homemade banners to the ballpark declaring their support for the team or a favorite player. Made mostly from bedsheets, some banners simply read, "Let's Go Mets!" Others were more creative, like the two-year-old boy holding a sign which read, "I've been a Mets fan all my life!" Bringing a banner to the ballpark to express your support for the team became so popular that the Mets eventually held their first "Banner Day" promotion back in 1963. Between games of a doubleheader, fans would parade on the field displaying their creations. Prizes were awarded to those banners judged to be the most creative in certain categories, such as "single-person banners," "banners held by two people," and so forth. Interestingly, true to their conservative image, the Yankees did not allow their fans to bring banners into Yankee Stadium back then. Today, however, fans' banners are a fixture in virtually every major league and minor league ballpark in the country, a baseball tradition that I believe was started by those loyal Mets fans back in 1962 at the old Polo Grounds.

Although I use the phrase "the old Polo Grounds" endearingly, the ballpark truly had seen better days. Since very little maintenance had been done in the years after the Giants vacated the Polo Grounds, a major drainage problem had developed at that once proud baseball shrine. With every heavy rain, the Harlem River would overflow and flood part of the outfield. I was told by my dear friend Johnny McCarthy, the first Mets' head groundskeeper, that the outfield was so bad one Sunday afternoon that the second game of a doubleheader had to be canceled due to flooding. And rumor also has it that one of the grounds crew actually used a rowboat that day to help drain the outfield after the crowd left the ballpark!

Bob Mandt, a dear friend of mine who is still with the Mets organization as a vice president, once told me another interesting story about the old Polo Grounds. Bob was in the ticket department in those early days and sold tickets at the Penn Station ticket office in midtown Manhattan. According to Bob, one of the biggest dilemmas faced by the Mets was determining whether all of the new seats had been put into the refurbished Polo Grounds. A physical count was never done to determine whether every printed ticket corresponded to an actual seat. This question was answered the first time the two Willies (Mays and McCovey) and the Giants came to town to play the Mets in May of 1962. The game was sold out that day, and thankfully there was a seat for every ticket holder!

When the committee was formed in 1960 to bring National League Baseball back to New York City, you could sense that the effort would be successful. The committee, which was chaired by Mayor Robert Wagner, included the former general manager of the Brooklyn Dodgers, Branch Rickey, and other prominent New Yorkers, among whom was attorney Bill Shea.

When the National League first turned down the expansion proposal, it was Shea who led the way for a new league. He wanted to call it the Continental League. When the president of the National League, Warren Giles, saw that Shea and his group were serious, they immediately welcomed two new expansion teams into the National League: the Houston Colt .45s and the New York Metropolitan Baseball Club, more affectionately known today as the Mets.

Many a story has been told about the Mets in those early days. One of my favorite tales involves the legendary Marvelous Marv Throneberry—a man who was born, dare I say destined, to be a Met in those early years. He personified all of the hopes and frustrations Mets fans would come to experience during that introductory 1962 campaign. In fact, the initials of his name even spell "Met" … Marvin Eugene Throneberry!

At one time, Throneberry had been a highly touted first-base prospect for the Yankees. However, by the time the Mets secured his services in 1962, Marv's reputation as a baseball player had diminished. But what Marv lacked in talent, he more than made up for in determination and desire.

It was a summer afternoon in 1962 at the Polo Grounds. The Mets were playing a doubleheader against the Cubs and had sold out the ballpark. Marv got up with the bases loaded and hit a tremendous triple more than 450 feet into the well area in deep center field, putting the Mets ahead for the first time all afternoon. There was Marv, standing proudly on third base in front of a cheering and appreciative crowd not accustomed to such heroics from the Mets in those early years. The umpires, however, ruled that Marv had not only missed first base but had also missed second base! The late Tom Gorman, who was to become one of my dearest friends in baseball, was the umpire-in-chief and was also working behind home plate that day. The way Tom told the story, the other umpires came over to him to discuss the matter. They all agreed. Throneberry had missed both first and second bases. No doubt about it. However, most of the discussion centered around who was going to tell Casey Stengel. As umpire-in-chief, that unenviable task fell to Tom. But when he called Casey over to inform him of Marv's infraction, expecting a good, old-fashioned tongue lashing from Stengel, all Casey had to say was, "Well, I know he didn't miss third base, 'cause he's standing on it!"

Another classic story about those early years with the Mets involved Jimmy Piersall. Piersall, a strong defensive center fielder and better-than-average hitter, was immortalized in the film, *Fear Strikes Out*. He had fought emotional problems most of his baseball life. Piersall was nearing the end of his baseball career in 1962 and had warned everyone that he was going to celebrate hitting his hundredth career home run by running the bases backwards. And he did! The fans and players loved it. Everyone except Stengel. Jimmy was gone not too long after that incident. The message was clear—if there was any clowning around to do, Casey would do it himself.

One of the strangest tales in the history of Mets baseball, perhaps in all of baseball, involved a little-known player of marginal talent, Harry Chiti. In 1962, Harry was traded by the Mets to the Cleveland Indians for a "player to be named later," which subsequently turned out to be … Harry Chiti! I think he was the only player in baseball history ever to be traded for himself. Once again, as Casey Stengel would say, "You could look it up!"

In 1963–64, the organization was ready to make the big move to their new ballpark in Flushing. The Mets were only supposed to play at the Polo Grounds for a year. But several problems developed over in Flushing, not the least of which was bad weather, which caused major plumbing problems at the new facility.

When season tickets were being sold in 1963 before the new ballpark was completed, only the grounds crew actually knew the configuration of the stadium. They would put wooden stakes on the field so that those of us in sales could show prospective season ticket buyers where their seats would be relative to the infield and outfield. The unusual idea worked; we sold over one million tickets that year!

One of the major selling points about the new ballpark in Flushing was its seating configuration. Most of the major league ballparks had been built early in the twentieth century. Conforming to the construction techniques of the day, large steel columns, or "poles," as they were affectionately called by the fans, supported each deck. When purchasing tickets, fans would invariably insist that they not be seated behind a pole, which could obstruct their view of the play on the field. The Mets' new stadium in Flushing incorporated modern construction techniques that eliminated the need for support poles. Every fan could now have an unobstructed view of virtually the entire playing field, an expectation today's fans take for granted when going to the ballpark.

The new stadium was at first called Flushing Memorial Stadium. This was soon changed to William A. Shea Stadium, named after the man who was responsible for bringing National League baseball back to New York. Regrettably, Bill passed away in 1991.

I will never forget the story Bill loved to tell whenever he made a public appearance. It seems that shortly after the stadium opened, Bill was coming into New York City from his home on Long Island. He was traveling on the Long Island Railroad, which passes right by Shea Stadium. As the train passed the stadium and the adjoining grounds of the World's Fair, two young men were having a discussion about the Mets—what else? As they passed the stadium, one said to the other, "By the way, who is this guy Shea, anyway?" The other quickly responded, "Oh, I think he's some guy who got killed in World War II, so they named a stadium after him." Bill would always end his speech by telling his audience, "It's called Shea Stadium ... not Shea Memorial Stadium!"

Looking back at the Mets' leadership in those early days, you sensed that success was just a matter of time. The owner, Mrs. Joan Payson, who was just as much a fan as she was an owner, fostered a sincere feeling of family among everyone throughout the organization. She and Chairman of the Board M. Donald Grant convinced George Weiss, former president and general manager of the New York Yankees, and Casey Stengel, Weiss' highly successful field manager, to come out of retirement and join the new organization. Stengel had led the New York Yankees to seven World Series championships and ten pennants in twelve years! And hopes were high that he would be able to establish a strong baseball franchise for New York's new National League entry as well. In 1961, Jim Thomson was chosen to handle the business end of the New York Mets organization. Jim had started with the Brooklyn Dodgers as an electrician and groundskeeper and then worked with George Weiss when George joined the New York Yankees.

An experienced front office, led by Jim Thomson on the business side and George Weiss on the baseball end, was now in place. To assist with player development, Weiss went back to his Yankee roots and hired the great Yankee reliever Johnny Murphy, who came to the organization with a well-earned reputation for successfully scouting young talent. In 1961, former legendary sportswriter Tom Meany also joined the Mets to handle promotions and public relations.

In the beginning of the franchise's history, the Mets drafted several fading, but nonetheless popular Brooklyn Dodgers stars. Players like All-Star first baseman Gil Hodges, All-Star center fielder Duke Snider, and infielders Charlie Neal and Don Zimmer were all drafted because of their gate appeal among old-time Brooklyn Dodgers fans, despite their diminished baseball skills. In addition, Murphy's goal was to establish a farm system that would eventually create a winning franchise on the major league level from within the organization.

One of Murphy's early prospects, and one of my favorite players, was Larry Bearnarth, out of St. John's University in Queens, New York. Larry worked mostly out of the bullpen. He was a natural leader for what was to become a very young pitching staff. Young pitchers like Dennis Ribant, Dick Selma, and Bill Wakefield were soon to follow. Although most of these young players met with limited major league success, the foundation of the farm system that would ultimately bring players like Tom Seaver, Buddy Harrelson, Jerry Koosman, and Nolan Ryan to the major leagues was now firmly in place. The stage had been set for the big move to Shea Stadium in 1964, a year late but well worth the wait.

Despite their ineptness and losing ways, the Mets drew well over one million fans each of their two seasons at the Polo Grounds (1962–63) and were the talk of the baseball world.

Of course, it was no secret that Casey Stengel had plenty to do with the team's success and popularity. But getting National League baseball back to New York was also a big factor. The city had always been a strong National League town, having supported two National League teams, the Brooklyn Dodgers and the New York Giants, for well over fifty years. Consequently, when the schedules for the upcoming seasons came out, most of the ticket requests were, quite naturally, for games against the Dodgers and Giants. The Mets seemed to win over most of the old Dodgers fans. But as long as Willie Mays and Willie McCovey were still playing for the Giants, New York Giants fans seemed to remain loyal to their old team.

I became Mr. Met, baseball's first mascot, in 1964. My job
was to entertain our young fans. Mr. Met was an instant
success with the home crowd.

With the move to Shea Stadium in 1964, quite a few changes
needed to be made within the organization. The attendance figures
were strong, so the major goal was to develop a contending team as
soon as possible. The World's Fair and Casey Stengel combined to be
a great draw for the fans. But the Mets organization realized early on
that New York is a baseball town and expected a winner soon. After
all, on the other side of town was a team called the Yankees. And they
had had New York all to themselves for a few years. It was now time
to change all that.

Despite being the most losing team in baseball, the Mets and their
millions of loyal fans moved to Shea Stadium in 1964 with great
hopes for a very bright and successful future. The move, however, was
not easy logistically. The maintenance and grounds crews were the
first to relocate to the new stadium. The executive offices remained at

Fifth Avenue, but a small facility was temporarily set up at a hotel near the new stadium for select office staff. A few ticket office people were moved over to Shea Stadium, but the conditions were outrageously bad. There were chemical toilets, tiny heating units, and not a restaurant to be found. Across the street you could see what was going to be the World's Fair, but there was never anyone in sight.

If we were worried about our upcoming Opening Day in 1964, we could just imagine what was going on across the way in what is now Flushing Meadows Park. The winter of 1963–64 was snowy and very cold, less than ideal conditions for outside construction. But everyone managed to get their jobs done. Shea Stadium and the 1964–65 World's Fair made their debuts, as scheduled, and the stage was set for some unforgettable baseball memories.

Let's Go Mets!

Chapter Two
From the Marines
to the Mets

It was on the beautiful tiny island of Guam, some nine thousand miles from New York City, that I started receiving some very unusual (and unbelievable) news articles from my mother back home in Queens, New York. There I was, a young Marine defending our western shores (although the time was post-Korea and pre-Vietnam), and all I was reading about was the pending move of the Brooklyn Dodgers and New York Giants to Los Angeles and San Francisco respectively. The distressing news clippings started arriving in 1957, and despite my hopes and prayers to the contrary, the long-rumored desertion became a reality in 1958, around the time I was transferred to Hawaii. This was all too much for me to take. As a Dodgers fan, I had already gone through enough abuse from Yankees fans back home in New York when Don Larsen pitched his famous World Series perfect game in 1956. And now this?

When I finally received my honorable discharge and returned home to New York City in 1959, reality had set in. Sure enough, the only game in town now belonged to the Yankees. And the "other guys" were playing out on the West Coast. We did hear an occasional rumor about a National League team leaving their city and moving to New York, but that never came about. Incredibly, National League President Warren Giles thought that the league would get along fine without a New York team. He obviously believed having just the Yankees in New York City representing the American League was more than enough baseball for any town.

As I said earlier, the committee that was formed to right this wrong and get National League baseball back to New York was led by prominent attorney Bill Shea. Essentially, Shea and his group threatened to form the new Continental League, and a number of large cities were ready to participate. That put a bit of a scare into Giles and the rest of the National League hierarchy. So the league agreed to add two new franchises, Houston and New York, to their line-up. The Houston franchise was originally called the Colt .45's and later became the Astros. The New York franchise was named the Metropolitan Baseball Club of New York, known then and today as the New York Mets.

While all this excitement was going on around baseball in New York in 1962, I was beginning a new career in the airline industry as a customer service representative for Northeast Airlines and subsequently for Scandinavian Airlines in New York City. In the spring of 1962, I joined with a few friends from different airlines to take advantage of our travel pass privileges and go down to Florida and meet the Mets.

When we arrived in Florida, we were all excited. The Mets were scheduled to play the Yankees in Ft. Lauderdale the next day. Led by the "M & M Boys," Roger Maris and Mickey Mantle, the Yankees had won the World Series against the Dodgers the year before. Maris had broken Babe Ruth's single-season home run record with sixty-one dingers in 1961. And "the Mick," Mickey Mantle, had also chased Ruth's record the year before, completing the 1961 season with fifty-four home runs.

I was convinced that the game was going to be a sellout. After all, it was the upstart New York Mets against the legendary New York Yankees. I had already purchased tickets for the group but felt we should get to the park early to beat the traffic and get a good parking space. So at my suggestion, we left our motel at 10:30 a.m. and arrived at the ballpark two hours before game time. To everyone's surprise, the parking lot was completely empty except for the stadium staff. To add to my embarrassment, when I asked the attendant at the parking lot where the crowd was, he said flippantly, "Oh, the Yankees are only playing the Mets today. Nobody around here has even heard of them." To no one's surprise, the Yankees beat the Mets that day. But little did we know that the loss was just a preview of what was waiting for the rest of New York when the team came north in the spring of 1962. Was Gotham really ready for this?

Baseball greats Roy Campanella, Gil Hodges, and Casey Stengel get together for an Old-Timers' Game. Casey was the Mets' first manager, and Gil brought the team its first World Series championship.

Friends have often asked me where the now famous "Let's Go Mets!" cheer started. I can't say for sure. But before the advent of the Mets in 1962, it was not common for baseball fans to cheer on the home team with a rhythmic, unison chant, not even at Ebbets Field in Brooklyn or Wrigley Field in Chicago. But during that spring-training game against the Yankees back in 1962, my friends and I, out of frustration, started chanting that refrain every time a Mets player came to the plate. "Let's Go Mets! Let's Go Mets!" It caught on almost immediately, and I vividly remember most of the fans in our section joining in. Little did we know that baseball history was being made that day. It was the first time I recall ever hearing any baseball fans cheer their team on this way. Today, at major league ballparks around the country, it's not uncommon to hear fans chant in unison, "Let's Go Yanks!" or "Let's Go Bucs!" However, I believe these cheers are the direct descendants of what was the first and arguably the most endearing baseball cheer of all, "Let's Go Mets!" So I guess my friends and I will take credit for its creation until someone comes along and proves differently.

Our loyalty to the Mets subsequently followed us north. Several of us attended about thirty to forty games that first season. And my job, naturally, was to get the tickets. That is how I got to know Bob Mandt. Bob had started his Mets career at their ticket outlet in Penn Station. We had known each other casually many years before, but school and the service separated us over time. Bob became our contact for Mets tickets in 1962.

What a great first year we had at the old Polo Grounds! Of course, we saw the legendary Marv Throneberry when he lost that "Ruthian" triple after missing both first and second bases. The sight of Jimmy Piersall running the bases backwards after hitting his hundredth career home run still brings a twinkle to my eye. And the collection of missed pop-ups, errant throws, and base running miscues that came to characterize the Mets in 1962 are all still fresh in my mind's eye. It seemed that every day the Mets would show their fans a new way to lose a ballgame. By the end of 1962, my friends and I had learned one hundred and twenty different ways to do just that, for the team managed to lose a record one hundred and twenty games, the most ever by a major league baseball team in a single season!

Hall of Famer Richie Ashburn, who had been an All-Star center fielder with the Philadelphia Phillies for many years, played center field for the Mets in 1962. During most of his illustrious career, Ashburn was overshadowed by the big three center fielders in New York: Mickey Mantle (Yankees), Willie Mays (Giants), and Duke Snider (Dodgers). But Ashburn was an outstanding defensive center fielder and a prolific lead-off hitter in his own right and truly deserved more recognition from the fans and media. Ashburn summed up his frustration with the Mets' maiden season succinctly when, after being told he was named "Most Valuable Met of 1962," he quipped, "That's nice. I was voted the most valuable player on the most losing team in baseball history!" And to add salt to the wound, the boat the Mets awarded Ashburn for being their MVP that year sank during its maiden voyage … just like the Mets during their initial campaign! Ashburn had seen enough and retired from baseball shortly thereafter to begin a long and illustrious career as a broadcaster for the Philadelphia Phillies. Richie passed away in 1998, just after broadcasting, strangely enough, a Phillies-Mets game at Shea Stadium.

In all fairness to the 1962 Mets, they had to face some pretty stiff pitching from Hall of Famers like Sandy Koufax, Don Drysdale, Juan Marichal, and Bob Gibson. You could argue that major league pitching today in general is better than it was back in 1962, especially with the recent emergence of dominating relief pitching. But there were only ten teams in the National League, not sixteen like today, so teams faced the likes of Koufax and company more often than they do today. And these future Hall of Fame pitchers prided themselves in their ability to go nine innings. There were times when we would go to the park for a game, look at the pitchers facing our guys, and say to ourselves, "This just isn't fair!" But in truth, the dominating pitchers of that era were not fair to National League hitters. It was a year none of us will ever forget.

The following year was filled with much more promise. In 1963, the Mets were to have moved to their new stadium in Flushing, but that was delayed a year due to construction problems. Nonetheless, when the 1963 season schedule came out and the tickets went on sale, I went over to see my buddy Bob Mandt at Penn Station to secure tickets for my friends and me. About halfway through the 1963 season, Bob and I had a conversation that eventually would change my life.

The airline career that I was pursuing had a very promising future. I was with Scandinavian Airlines and was in the process of being promoted to the sales department in New York City. It was at that time that Bob advised me that he was going to be promoted to ticket manager for the Mets once they moved into their new stadium. He realized even then that he would need to increase the department's staff and asked if I would be interested in a job with the Mets. I was flattered! And it didn't take me long to make the decision. Even though my future at Scandinavian Airlines looked bright, this was an opportunity to join a new and exciting organization. And of course, it involved baseball, which I obviously loved. And the thought of being part of the move to the new stadium, with the World's Fair directly across the street, made the decision that much easier.

A few days later, I told Bob that I was definitely interested in his offer, so he set up an interview for me with Jim Thomson, the Mets' business manager. The interview was scheduled for early February somewhere in the new ballpark. I repeat, "somewhere in the new ballpark," because the offices had yet to be built, except for a small area for the ticket department staff.

It was a cold, snowy day when I left my apartment in Queens for the interview. Normally, it was only about a twenty minute ride to the ballpark by subway. But with the snowstorm that day, it took me almost an hour. When I arrived at the Flushing Meadows IRT subway station, it was one of the loneliest and most gloomy sights I had ever seen in my life. On one side of the elevated subway tracks was a seemingly abandoned construction site that would later that year be miraculously transformed into the 1964–65 World's Fair. On the other side of the tracks was the unfinished stadium. And not a soul in sight! But you could hear the din of activity inside the ballpark. My first thought was, "I know it's only February, but will any of this be ready on time?"

I walked around the stadium and couldn't find a single door. Finally, I noticed a small opening, which looked a little like an entrance. As I walked through the opening, I saw two men sitting at a desk, dressed in large winter coats and trying to keep warm under somewhat trying conditions. Obviously, they were startled to see me wandering about in such weather. It turns out that they were members of Bob Mandt's staff from the Mets' ticket department, handling season subscribers and transfers from the Polo Grounds while sitting at a desk and trying to keep warm in the middle of a snowstorm.

I told them that I had an appointment with Jim Thomson. They certainly got a laugh out of that, because I had assumed that the offices at the stadium were ready. They immediately gave me the bad news: Jim Thomson and his staff were still at the Travelers Hotel, several miles away near LaGuardia Airport.

The new section of highway connecting the World's Fair and the ballpark to the Grand Central Parkway and LaGuardia was still under construction. And as yet, there was no mass transit linking the stadium to LaGuardia. So I had to make my way on foot through the snowstorm and subfreezing temperatures to the airport, some two miles away.

By the time I found the hotel, I was beginning to question both my sanity and whether or not this was all worth my while. My face was cold, my toes were freezing, and my clothes were soaked. I could have been back in my nice warm office at Scandinavian Airlines, taking advantage of my travel pass privileges and planning a trip to sunny Florida!

Inside the hotel, the Mets had set up a temporary switchboard with a few desks. Jim Thomson was running a little late supervising a major equipment move from the Polo Grounds to the new ballpark.

This transition move in itself was fascinating. The Mets organization consisted of an executive office in midtown Manhattan, a temporary office at the Travelers Hotel near LaGuardia Airport, and moving crews and grounds crews shuttling back and forth between the two ballparks. No wonder I couldn't find Jim Thomson.

When I finally did find him, Jim and I sat down and had a great conversation. This was no interview in the traditional sense. Jim made me feel very comfortable, very relaxed. As a result, I felt I had known this man for years. When I look back, I think Bob had already given Jim his approval for my hiring. We just had to decide what my position would be and, of course, my salary. Jim explained that I would have to take a slight pay cut from my airline salary. But he also convinced me that in the long run I would be making the right career decision. I agreed and accepted Jim's offer to join the Mets organization, working in the ticket department.

The Mets may have been the most losing team in baseball history their first two years, but with the excitement and interest generated by their new stadium, all that appeared to be behind them now. The fans had really fallen in love with the team at the Polo Grounds and supported them with strong attendance. I thought the upcoming 1964 season would be an exciting one, and I wanted to be a part of that excitement. I couldn't wait to get started!

Early Mets included shortstop Roy McMillan (51), outfielder
Frank Thomas (25), pitcher Al Jackson (15), and shortstop
Felix Mantilla (18).

I started my career with the Mets in late February 1964. On my
first day, I reported directly to Bob Mandt's office—which at the time
was also the main ticket office—for an explanation of my initial
duties. When I arrived, I saw a group of men, all sitting around
counting tickets. In that age before the computerization of the ticketing process, every ticket for every game had to be hand-counted and
matched to a corresponding seat in the stadium. This was a monu-
mental, around-the-clock undertaking, requiring the assistance of
part-time personnel who worked on the project after completing their
regular jobs. Looking back, I am amazed at how far we have come in
recent years, with the ticketing process dramatically facilitated and
automated today through the use of computers.

By March of 1964, I was the ticket seller at our Grand Central Station ticket office in New York City. However, prior to that, I had been assigned the job of showing potential season ticket holders their seat locations at Shea Stadium. That assignment was most enjoyable for me because the clients were so enthusiastic and anxious to see their seats. But it wasn't easy. Only about half of the seats were actually in place. In fact, they were still putting in seats and painting them right up to Opening Day! Because the playing field was still under construction, we would use the architect's drawing to show clients where their seats were located relative to home plate, first base, third base, the dugouts, and the outfield. Ultimately, John McCarthy, our head groundskeeper, marked each base with a spike so we could at least determine the exact location of the infield.

Those first few weeks with the Mets were really a special time for me. We were all in this exciting new adventure together. The veteran ticket salesmen from the Dodgers and Giants were just as new to this as we were. But without their selling experience, we would have had big problems.

Bob Mandt had put together a great staff of people. In fact, we were the talk of the league. Capacity crowds greeted each team as they came to town. And yet we still managed to do our job effectively and to keep everyone happy.

The veteran ticket salesmen who came over to the Mets from the old Brooklyn Dodgers and New York Giants were a great bunch of guys. And they all had such great stories to tell about "the old days" of baseball in New York. One of the most colorful of these characters was John McKee, who had worked for many years in the Brooklyn Dodgers' ticket office and was, at the time, one of my closest co-workers. Before I left for my assignment at the Grand Central Terminal ticket office, John and I had been unable to find an acceptable restaurant near Shea Stadium where we could relax, eat, drink, and just get away from the ballpark for a while. There was an Italian restaurant nearby owned by a very lovely couple who, as we later suspected, apparently had very limited experience in the restaurant business. A group of about six of us, including John, decided to go there one day for lunch. The restaurant happened to be very busy that day, so the owner's wife decided to help out by taking customers' orders herself, even though she had little, if any, waitressing experience. As luck would have it, she waited on our table. When it came time to order, everyone in our party ordered something different: a salad, hero sandwich, and so forth. John McKee ordered a hamburger cooked medium rare. When his burger arrived, he took one bite and immediately declared that it didn't taste quite right. So John called our waitress over and told her that his hamburger tasted funny. We all expected her either to take the burger back to the kitchen to reheat or to offer John either another burger or something else for his trouble. Instead, to our shock and amazement, she picked up the hamburger, took a healthy bite, placed it decisively back on John's plate, and matter-of-factly proclaimed to all before walking away, "There's nothing wrong with this hamburger!" Despite this bizarre episode, we continued to frequent the restaurant because of its convenience and proximity to Shea Stadium. And the food there really was actually quite good. But from that day on, we made it a point to eat at the bar whenever we could rather than dining at a table in order to avoid that waitress.

Chapter Three
Meet Mr. Met

The Mets organization opened its New York City ticket outlets in March 1964. I was assigned to work with a veteran ticket seller with Broadway theater experience, Ed Barker. This guy was right out of a Damon Runyon novel. None of us could be expected to know all of the seat locations at Shea Stadium. But Ed had a way of convincing most customers that their seats were practically in the dugout. As expected, Ed's unbridled enthusiasm sometimes created problems for us when customers returned to purchase tickets for another game.

While Ed and I were selling Mets tickets for the upcoming season in midtown Manhattan, seats were still being installed at Shea Stadium. It was around this time that Johnny McCarthy's grounds crew had decided to place stakes in the ground to help us show clients where their seats would be relative to the infield. It was late March 1964 and Opening Day was just about sold out. And since I lived in Queens, not far from Shea Stadium, I would volunteer to make the trip out to the ballpark to get more tickets for our Grand Central and Penn Station ticket offices. By early April, with less than two weeks until the 1964 home opener and Shea Stadium's debut, Opening Day was officially sold out. It didn't matter that construction of the new stadium had not yet been completed and a sizable number of seats had yet to be installed. To this day, I am convinced that Ed Barker's assurances of "right by the dugout seats" to many of our loyal Mets fans contributed significantly to this achievement.

Naturally, every time I made the trip out to Shea Stadium from midtown Manhattan, I had to get a World's Fair progress report. All indications were that construction was moving along smoothly, albeit slowly. But it still didn't look like the fair would be ready for its scheduled opener in April. That seemed to be the question on everybody's mind. Would both Shea Stadium and the World's Fair be ready to open their doors on time to an excited public?

With Opening Day completely sold out, naturally attention now focused on the next big gate attractions: the Los Angeles Dodgers and the San Francisco Giants. Willie Mays and Willie McCovey, as well as Juan Marichal, were all still with the Giants. And Mets fans could look forward to seeing the great Sandy Koufax and the equally intimidating Don Drysdale facing their team when the Dodgers came to town. Ticket sales for all upcoming games were on the rise. Was it the World's Fair, National League baseball, the new stadium, or the Mets ball club itself that generated all of this interest and excitement among New York baseball fans? Even though the team finished last in its first two seasons in the National League, the Mets enjoyed a remarkable love affair with New York. But if the truth be told, the team's strong attendance in 1964 was probably the result of all of the above factors.

During many of my ticket runs out to Shea Stadium, I ran into Tom Meany, who at the time was both publicity and promotion director for the Mets. Tom was an accomplished sportswriter and columnist in New York City. Every time I did my ticket runs, I made it a point to stop by Tom's office to talk baseball. About a week before the 1964 opener, Tom and I were in the middle of one such discussion, when he suddenly asked me if I would be available to assist him with the Opening Day ceremonies. He wanted to know if I would help him coordinate the day's festivities and participants, including the band, the Color Guard, the National Anthem singer, and several other activities.

I played the part of Mr. Met from 1964 to 1967. In 2006, I
posed at a party with the newest Mr. Met.

What a great opportunity! I was planning on coming to the ballpark that morning anyway. I just had to make arrangements with my
partner back at the ticket office to cover for me that afternoon so I
didn't have to go back to midtown Manhattan while the game was in
progress. For me, this was a dream come true. Imagine assisting an
accomplished sportswriter and baseball man like Tom Meany during
an historic event like the Mets' 1964 home opener and the debut of
Shea Stadium. I was thrilled!

It was April 17, 1964, when the New York Mets opened their season at spanking new Shea Stadium against the Pittsburgh Pirates. I
arrived at the ballpark just after 10 a.m. and reported immediately to
Tom's office. It was there that I met his secretary, Janice, and his assistant on the publicity side, John Geis. These two people were so help-

ful to me that day. I never will forget them. And to this day, both are treasured friends.

Tom Meany had a sizable and diverse list of duties that John was to coordinate that day. And John was relieved that I was available to assist him. John's primary focus was to address the needs of the vast media corps covering this historic event. I remember my first assignment was to meet the Armed Forces Color Guard at the press gate. After that, there was the Army Band, which was going to play the National Anthem. I walked with them all the way out to center field and beyond the fence to the flagpole to get them into position for their performance.

The view from center field at Shea Stadium, especially looking into the stands filled with fans, was breathtaking. It is amazing how major league outfielders are able to pick up fly balls amid that crowd of white shirts and banners! In fact, the great Willie Mays said on several occasions that Shea Stadium was the hardest center field he ever played, more difficult than even Candlestick Park, with its strong and tricky winds.

After getting the assorted military personnel settled in the outfield, I returned to the area behind home plate to meet the singer who was going to perform the National Anthem accompanied by the Army Band. He and his party were most gracious. I escorted them to their seats and directed him when it was time to go out onto the field. All of the festivities that day ran smoothly, I suspect, because most of the participants arrived on time or a little early. Tom Meany, however, had no such luck. He had to meet Mayor John Lindsay and several VIPs, all of whom got stuck in traffic and were late for the ceremonies.

After the first-pitch ceremonies were completed, it was time to play ball. So Tom, John, and I went upstairs to watch the game from the press level. Both men had game assignments with the press corps. But my job was finished for the day. So I was now able to relax, kick back, and just be a part of the excitement. I will never forget that day. Of course, we lost to the Pirates, 4 to 3, with slugging first baseman and future Hall of Famer Willie Stargell hitting the first Shea Stadium home run. Frank Thomas, a power-hitting left fielder and fan favorite, hit the first-ever Mets home run at Shea Stadium that same day. Frank had been obtained by the Mets from the Pirates organization in the 1961 expansion draft. He was a right-handed pull hitter who the Mets thought would do well at the old Polo Grounds, with its short, left-field fence only 255 feet from home plate. So as fate would have it, the Pirates organization was forever linked to the first home runs ever hit at Shea Stadium by both a Met and a visiting player!

With the home opener out of the way, the Mets went on with the rest of the season. The team's first solid young prospect was a second baseman by the name of Ron Hunt. Ron was a scrappy young player who played great defense and had a pretty good bat. His ability to get on base, either by walking or getting hit by a pitch, was the talk of the league. And Ron always stayed after batting practice to sign autographs and talk to the fans. As a result, he was a very popular player. In 1964, the Mets had quite a few fan-accessible players. In addition to Hunt, there were Jim Hickman, Rod Kanehl, Chris Cannizzaro, Al Jackson, and Larry Bearnarth. I believe that was another reason for the team's popularity and the strong attendance that year. Hunt proudly represented the Mets at the 1964 All-Star Game played at Shea Stadium, the first and only time to date that the Mets have hosted the All-Star classic. Hunt was also the first Mets player ever to be voted as a starter to an All-Star team and was runner-up in Rookie of the Year honors in 1964, losing out to a fellow by the name of Pete Rose. So, even though the Mets had another losing season, the future was beginning to look brighter. Mets fans began to sense this and stuck with the team all the way.

I'm sure that both the new ballpark and the World's Fair across the street had a large part to do with the baseball commissioner's decision to play the 1964 All-Star Game in New York City. Of course, that meant that the Mets were the host team. And the responsibilities for Tom Meany, his staff, and of course Bob Mandt and the rest of us in the ticket department, were enormous. The game was scheduled to be played at Shea Stadium on the afternoon of July 7. As usual, I opened the ticket office in Manhattan and left for the ballpark as soon as my partner Ed arrived. When I got to the stadium, Tom Meany had the entire schedule mapped out for each of us. What a memorable day!

Up to that point in my young career, I had never been in the clubhouse. But Tom made it a point of taking me with him to meet the players and to review with them their pregame introductions. We went into both clubhouses, which for that one day were identified as "National League All-Stars" and "American League All-Stars" instead of the usual "Mets" and "Visitors" clubhouses. As I followed Tom around, I was introduced to many of the baseball greats of that era, players like Stan Musial, Willie Mays, Sandy Koufax, and Mickey Mantle, just to name a few. I was in awe of them. Yet I tried to act as cavalier and professional as possible. However, in all my excitement, I am sure there were players I was introduced to that day whom I still don't remember meeting. As Tom introduced me to various front office personnel from several of the other major league clubs, I began to feel welcomed and very comfortable with the baseball community. As I look back on that memorable day, I realize that Tom really didn't need me to walk around the clubhouses with him. He had everything under control. Instead, this was a little thank-you for helping him out on Opening Day and the All-Star Game.

Manager Casey Stengel, *center*, is surrounded by five other
Mets: *back row, left to right*, coach Wes Westrum, outfielder
Frank Thomas and pitcher Carl Willey; *front row*, pitchers
Jay Hook and Al Jackson. I directed the Speakers Bureau for
the Mets. Hook and Jackson were two of the best
spokespersons for the team.

After the 1964 All-Star break, the Mets organization turned its
attention back to National League baseball in New York City and the
resumption of an exciting season. One day shortly after the break,
Tom Meany called me at the ticket office in midtown Manhattan and
told me that the Mets' business manager, Jim Thomson, wanted to
see us both in his office the next day. I couldn't imagine what this
could be about, and Tom wasn't giving me a clue. The night before
my meeting with Jim certainly seemed to last forever. I was so nervous
I couldn't sleep. None of us had any idea what the promotional plans
were for the next year. So I thought perhaps that was the reason for

the meeting with Jim. Helping Tom Meany with next year's promotion plans certainly couldn't hurt my chances of working with him in an expanded capacity in the future. However, I assumed that I would stay in the ticket department with Bob and his staff. I met with Tom Meany and Jim Thomson in Jim's office first thing the next morning. As Tom and I waited outside for his secretary to announce us, I noticed, and I found this to be true in the years to come, that Jim's door was wide open. He waved for us to come in and sit down. Jim had a great-looking office, stocked with all sorts of baseball memorabilia from his old Brooklyn Dodger and New York Yankee days. And he was the type of person who made you feel comfortable right away. Jim and I had met only once before, during my job interview with the Mets. Yet I was very comfortable in his presence.

Early on in our meeting, Jim pointed to some baseball items on his desk—a ticket stub from a previous game, some Mets stationery, and several Mets souvenirs—and asked me if I noticed anything that these items had in common. The answer was obvious. All of the items had that cute little Mr. Met caricature printed on them. We then went on to talk about the youthful following the Mets appeared to be developing. Jim felt these younger fans were being introduced to the Mets by their parents, who themselves had been fans of the Brooklyn Dodgers and New York Giants. And the fact that there was an ever-growing number of younger Mets fans appeared to be reinforced by the overwhelming sales of souvenirs with the Mr. Met caricature printed on them.

I then realized the reason for our meeting. Jim and Tom had discussed the possibility of creating a live Mr. Met to greet and entertain our young fans when they came out to the ballpark. This would be a first for major league baseball. Team mascots had been widely used in college sports for years, but not in the major leagues. Mr. Met would be the first team mascot in major league baseball history. Little did we realize how ingenious this concept was. Mr. Met would forever change the experience of going to a major league baseball game for fans of all ages nationwide. The concept would spawn popular baseball mascots like the San Diego Chicken and the Phillie Phanatic. As with the innovative "Let's Go Mets!" cheer, the New York Mets organization was once again about to leave its mark on major league baseball history.

Some purists might contend that the first team mascot in major league baseball was actually a little-known beagle named Homer. This diminutive canine, the brainchild of the New York Mets' sponsor Rheingold Beer, could be found behind home plate during each home game at the old Polo Grounds. The loveable pooch literally did nothing but sit there. But the fact is, Homer was a mascot for Rheingold Beer, not the Mets. So technically, he was not truly a team mascot. In subsequent years, Charlie Finley, owner of the Kansas City Athletics, would also adopt a team mascot, a live mule named Charlie-O that was paraded onto the field before each home game. Homer and Charlie-O never really caught on with the fans. Nonetheless, Homer was the first effort, failed or otherwise, at some type of mascot in major league baseball. And once again, it was an attempt at innovation developed early on by the New York Mets franchise.

Jim asked me if I would be interested in taking on the project. It would involve me dressing up as Mr. Met and entertaining our young fans at the ballpark. I suspected all along that Tom had recommended me to Jim, since I was always willing to take on additional responsibilities, no questions asked. Also, I think Jim realized I had a little bit of ham in me and would therefore be very receptive to the idea. In truth, I was a little concerned about how this assignment would affect my aspirations as an up-and-coming baseball executive. In the end, however, I eagerly accepted the challenge, no questions asked.

Shortly after our initial meeting, Tom and I were once again back in Jim's office to follow up on the Mr. Met project. This time, however, we had a visitor joining us. It was a huge papier-mâché head in the form of a baseball with a bright, smiling face. "Try it on, Dan," said Jim, with that big toothy grin of his. Tom Meany stood off to the side of the room, holding back his laughter. Meany, a man who had seen some of the greatest sports legends of all time—Ruth, DiMaggio, great boxers like Joe Louis and Jack Dempsey—could now add the birth of baseball's first mascot, Mr. Met, to his illustrious list of sports memories.

I gingerly put on the oversized head, which was shaped like a giant baseball and had a bright, smiling face. I felt a little unsteady at first, but there was a sweatband inside the head to provide stability and a mesh screen mouth to see through. I put my arms through the straps and proceeded to stroll around the office comfortably and without any inhibitions. I did not realize that Jim had opened his office door so his staff could witness this historic event. Once I saw the reaction of everybody in the room, I knew Mr. Met was going to be a hit with the fans. All of my co-workers loved him. Of course, I still had my business suit on, without the jacket. How much that added to the frivolity of the moment, I'll never know. But I'm sure it didn't hurt!

The next order of business was to get me into a Mets baseball uniform to round out Mr. Met's persona. That wasn't too difficult, since back then I was in pretty good shape. I was assigned a genuine baseball uniform, just like the players', but without a number. Naturally, Jim asked all of us to keep Mr. Met under wraps until the details of his debut could be worked out. But I had to tell Bob Mandt. He and I had shared so many laughs together in the past that I just couldn't wait to see his reaction. When I told Bob about the project, he simply laughed and said, "Of all the people to choose from, Dan, they got the right guy with you!"

Bob Mandt had an assistant handling season ticket requests and priority orders. His name was Bill Gibson. Bill was affectionately known as "the Judge." He came to the Mets from the Dodgers organization, where he had sold tickets at their outlet on Montague Street in Brooklyn. That office was not far from the downtown area where most of the courthouses were located. Many of Bill's best customers were lawyers, court officers, and judges. And that's why he was nicknamed "the Judge" by his co-workers in Brooklyn. I don't think there was a more colorful character in the Mets organization, and maybe all of baseball, than the Judge. You never knew what the guy would say in public, especially after a busy day at the ballpark. Once he reportedly said to a fan who had asked for tickets to either a Giants or Dodgers game, "If Christ himself were to walk through that door right now wanting tickets to those games, I would have to tell him to go to hell." I will never forget Bill's reaction when he first saw Mr. Met. It reminded him of those crazy days with the Dodgers back in Brooklyn. He often told me that Mr. Met would have fit in perfectly with that Dodgers crowd. I took that as a compliment and still another indication that Mr. Met was going to catch on big with the fans.

The date for Mr. Met's debut at Shea Stadium had yet to be decided. But one thing was certain: unlike today's baseball mascots, who entertain fans virtually nonstop between innings, Mr. Met was to be less obtrusive. His appearances would be limited to pregame ceremonies and the break between games of a doubleheader. It was decided that Mr. Met would be introduced to Shea Stadium fans between the games of a Sunday doubleheader against the Giants in May. We tried to keep this decision a secret, but that was easier said than done. John McCarthy and his grounds crew found out about Mr. Met, since I kept his head and uniform near their storage area. By the time Mr. Met made his debut in May 1964, I suspect that most everyone in the Mets organization had heard rumors about his existence and were eagerly awaiting his arrival.

The eventful day finally arrived. The doubleheader with the Giants was almost a sellout. The sun was shining brightly against a Met-blue sky. And the crowd was excited about seeing the Giants back in New York. It was a perfect day for Mr. Met's debut. Tom Meany was excited. Jim Thomson kept wishing me well. Their instructions to me were really quite simple: just go out there and ad lib, shake the fans' hands, wave to the crowd, and sign autographs for the kids. I was certainly ready, as ready as I ever would be. But were the roughly fifty thousand fans attending the doubleheader that Sunday afternoon ready? We were about to find out.

Chapter Four
Mr. Met:
The Adventure Begins

I reported to Tom Meany's office that morning with a considerable amount of trepidation. Yes, I was excited about performing as Mr. Met and entertaining our fans, especially the younger ones, and yes, I had willingly turned my back on what I thought could be a promising career in sales with the Mets organization to attempt something no one had ever tried before. We were in uncharted waters. No one had any idea how the fans and media would react to Mr. Met. Would he be embraced as the loveable symbol of New York Mets baseball we all thought he could be? Or would he be laughed off the field as a silly joke?

I had received very specific yet limited direction from Mets' management regarding Mr. Met's choreography on the field. I was simply to greet our fans, particularly the young ones, and wave to them cheerfully. In brief, I was to be a real-life version of the familiar Mr. Met caricature, nothing more. Subsequent baseball mascots like the San Diego Chicken and Phillie Phanatic would expand upon this considerably and, in my opinion, for the better. Mr. Met's successful introduction assured these later mascots that fans would accept and enjoy their acts at the ballpark. This, in turn, allowed them the creative freedom to choreograph and expand their characters' own unique and entertaining personas. Subsequent baseball mascots were much more animated and choreographed, included more physical comedy in their routines and were given considerably more time to entertain the fans at the ballpark. But back in 1964, no one honestly knew how Mr. Met would be received by the fans and media. We also had no idea that he would forever change the marketing of the game of baseball.

When I arrived at the ballpark that sunny Sunday morning, Tom Meany asked me to go directly to the Mets' clubhouse. Just outside the clubhouse door would be a large carton with the words "Mr. Met" printed on the outside. My costume would be in that box. I was to see Herb Norman, our clubhouse manager, about using his facilities to suit up and get into character as Mr. Met. Herb would be expecting me.

I went to the clubhouse and, as arranged, Herb Norman was there waiting for me. I had met Herb on several previous occasions. He was a great guy who had been around baseball and football for many years. His responsibilities were considerable. Not only was he in charge of the players' uniforms (home and away) but also all of their equipment. I was obviously very nervous that first day, and Herb was a great comfort. He told me that all the players had heard about Mr. Met and were looking forward to seeing him perform. After all, as I realized later, they were fathers also and were excited about seeing how their children would react to Mr. Met and his antics. Herb placed my costume in one of the empty lockers in a remote corner of the clubhouse. All I could do now was wait for the moment of my big debut. So I nervously made my way upstairs to join Tom Meany in the press box for the start of the first game.

To my surprise, Tom took me to the press room for lunch before the game. While there, he introduced me to two of the most accomplished sports writers covering the Mets, Maury Allen of the *New York Post* (currently syndicated in Rockland County) and Dick Young of the *New York Daily News*. Dick was a true Mets fan. He would routinely quote Casey Stengel's famous "Amazin' Mets" and "You could look it up" adages in his newspaper columns. Dick was also responsible for coining the phrase "the New Breed" to differentiate enthusiastic Mets fans from the old-guard, conservative Yankee fans of the day. Meeting these two giants of sports journalism that eventful day helped me to relax and get my mind off Mr. Met's imminent debut, even if just briefly.

The team's original owner, Mrs. Joan Payson, was loved by everyone in the organization. Here she chats with her all-time favorite player, Hall of Famer Willie Mays.

The press room at most major league ballparks was essentially a working dining room where reporters worked on their stories for next day's publication. So visiting the press room at Shea Stadium was a real behind-the-scenes treat for me, an experience I will never forget. Other members of both the media and baseball establishment also took advantage of the press room's facilities. These included executives from both the visiting and home clubs as well as radio and TV personnel. As a result, that was the first time I met the three original Mets TV and radio announcers: Hall of Famer Ralph Kiner, Lindsey Nelson, and my dear friend Bob Murphy. Little did I know how closely I would get to work with these three fine gentlemen in the years to come. But for now, it was obvious that no one in the press room, including Kiner, Nelson, and Murphy, had any idea about Mr. Met's debut. I was there just to assist Tom Meany with some promotional activity. Or so they thought.

Tom and I left the press room and proceeded along the press level at Shea to a small section behind home plate. This was Tom's base of operations. In the booth were at least three electricians powering the large scoreboard in right center field, the public address system, and the organ. This room was often called the operations booth. The electricians were responsible for putting fan messages on the scoreboard and displaying the current batter's balls and strikes, as well as outs in the inning and out-of-town scores. The public address announcer was Jack Lee, son of the late Mike Lee, sports editor for the old *Long Island Press* newspaper. Jack subsequently left the Mets to pursue a career calling harness races at local New York metropolitan tracks. Another very special person in the booth that day was Jane Jarvis, organist for the New York Mets. Jane, who later became a very dear friend of mine, came to the Mets from the Milwaukee Braves organization. In the years to come, I would affectionately refer to them as my "friends in the booth." However, it was on the day of Mr. Met's debut that we were first introduced to one another.

Shortly after arriving in the booth, Tom asked me to assist him with the out-of-town scores. When a major league score came over the ticker tape, I would convey it verbally to the electrician in charge. This, of course, would include any pitching changes. It was a relatively easy assignment, but it required my complete and undivided attention to what was coming in over that tape.

It was during the sixth inning of the first game when I realized that the moment of truth was about to arrive. It was now time for me to go downstairs to the clubhouse to prepare for Mr. Met's debut. So I said good-bye to my new friends in the booth and headed for the clubhouse. I was hoping Herb Norman would be there alone to greet me. But no such luck. The Mets were playing a doubleheader that day, and several players were there preparing for the second game.

The first player to greet me was Rod Kanehl, also known as Hot Rod. Rod was one of the most versatile players in Mets history. He was willing to play any position, and almost did. Casey loved him for his ability and spirit, and so did the fans. Like Ron Hunt, Kanehl was another one of those young Mets players who would stay after both batting practice and games to sign autographs for the fans.

Another player in the clubhouse that memorable day was Chris Cannizzaro, arguably the franchise's first potential All-Star catcher. Although he was a light hitter, Chris had a great arm and handled the team's young pitching staff with authority. The Mets had gone through a number of catchers in those early years. However, Chris, with his considerable defensive skills behind the plate, appeared to have nailed down that important position. There was one small problem, however. Casey Stengel could not pronounce Cannizzaro's name! Whenever Casey talked to the press about his ball club, he would refer to his catcher as Chris Cannzoneri, not Cannizzaro. It was always Cannzoneri this and Cannzoneri that. Chris, a class guy all the way, just accepted it and gave Casey yet another opportunity to entertain both the press and fans.

It was late in the first game. And of course, we were losing, which didn't make me feel any better. I was concerned about Mr. Met making his historical debut after a loss in front of a virtually sold-out crowd. However, over the years I would get used to that. With the amount of games the Mets lost, I had no choice. So I put on my Mets uniform, gingerly grabbed Mr. Met's large round baseball head, and nervously started out the clubhouse door. Rod Kanehl and Chris Cannizzaro were still in the Mets clubhouse, along with a young pitching prospect by the name of Bill Wakefield. With a straight face, they asked me to put on my Mr. Met head. Well, I shrugged my shoulders and thought to myself, "Why not? I've got to do this sooner or later." So I placed that seam-laced baseball head squarely over my shoulders and into position. Their reaction was just what I needed to boost my confidence. They immediately laughed, good-naturedly of course, and wished me luck. Wakefield may not have had any children at the time, but Kanehl and Cannizzaro couldn't wait to see their children's reaction to Mr. Met.

I proceeded to the area behind home plate, where Johnny McCarthy, Pete Flynn, Joey Costello, and the rest of the Shea Stadium grounds crew were getting ready to go on the field to prepare it for the second game. The Mets were losing by a couple of runs, with two out in the bottom of the ninth. We were all standing there patiently waiting for the inevitable. Sure enough, the third out mercifully arrived, and the game was finally over. The Mets had lost another one. Immediately and without any warning, the gate behind home plate swung open and the grounds crew hurried onto the field to begin preparing it for the second game. As they whisked by me, the guys winked, whistled, and wished me luck. I was now on my own, with nothing more than a sinking feeling in my stomach and an oversized baseball on my head.

I stepped out onto the sun-drenched field that day without any predetermined ideas of how I could entertain a crowd of fifty thousand screaming baseball fans who had just seen their team lose to the hated Giants. Instinctively, I headed towards friendly territory, the Mets' dugout along the first-base side. I figured I would be safe there. I began waving to the fans in the field boxes when, to my surprise, they began waving back. Next thing I knew, a horde of young fans swarmed down to the railing near the Mets' dugout to greet me! I signed autographs and posed for several photos. But the fans, particularly the very young ones, were fascinated by Mr. Met's head. "How do you see out of that thing?" they asked repeatedly. Feeling more comfortable and daring, I crossed home plate and wandered over to the third-base side, where the fans' reception was just as enthusiastic. I could finally relax and enjoy the moment. Mr. Met's debut was a success!

There were only about twenty to thirty minutes between games of a doubleheader, so Mr. Met's inaugural appearance went quickly. I stayed on the field to entertain the fans as long as I could. However, when the players came out to warm up for the second game, I knew it was time for me to make my exit. But the ballplayers had other ideas. Seeing me for the first time, several of them began knocking on my head playfully. As I turned around to see who was trying to get my attention, another player would jokingly tap my head from behind, causing me to turn yet again. This went on for several minutes, and the fans loved it. Other players decided to toss a few baseballs my way to test my vision. I held out my arms hoping to catch a ball or two. But all I caught was a stream of baseballs hitting me squarely on the forehead. Once again, the fans howled with delight. It was all in good fun. And everyone seemed to enjoy the spontaneity of the moment.

By now, however, I was anxious to learn how Jim, Tom, and the rest of my co-workers felt about Mr. Met's debut. Scurrying off the field and into the clubhouse, I decided to take a shower in the players' room before seeking out Jim and Tom in the press level. I must admit, that felt a little odd. Somehow, I didn't feel like I belonged in there. But when Herb Norman stopped by to give me a cold can of Rheingold beer, one of our more popular sponsors, I knew I had arrived!

I dressed hurriedly and proceeded back up to the press level. Along the way, several members of the grounds crew and some of the special officers on duty in that area congratulated me on a job well done. Theirs was the first feedback I received from my co-workers, and thankfully it was positive. I truly appreciated their kind words and told them so. It meant that Mr. Met's initial appearance was a success and that everybody enjoyed the enthusiasm of our young fans. Among that contingent was the head groundskeeper, John McCarthy, who passed away in 1993; Pete Flynn, who has since assumed John's responsibilities; and Joe Costello, who is currently in charge of the executive entrance at Shea Stadium. To this day, Pete and Joe still call me Mr. Met.

Back at the booth, I was met with a mixture of applause and humorous barbs. Tom Meany was smiling at all the attention I was receiving, and I could tell he was very proud of my performance and me. He kept telling me how great it was to see all those young fans enjoying themselves with Mr. Met. It was obviously a successful promotion. But how did Jim Thomson feel about Mr. Met's initial performance? For me, his response to the day's festivities was most crucial. I looked over to Jim's booth on the other side of home plate, but I could not discern his reaction one way or another. He was chatting, stone-faced, with a gentleman whom I could not recognize. Jim never showed any emotion. But if there was anything wrong, he was the kind of guy who would let you know right away. About the seventh inning of the second game, Jim called Tom and asked us to meet him after the game in the Diamond Club, a restaurant and bar used exclusively by our season ticket holders. Many of us in the Mets organization would also meet there on occasion after a game to conduct business or simply socialize with the press and fans. So Jim's invitation was not out of the ordinary.

Jim arrived for our meeting on time and gave no hint of his feelings about Mr. Met's introduction earlier that day. He didn't have to. Apparently, while watching the second game, Jim was visited in his booth by several members of the press corps, who had nothing but good things to say about Mr. Met. Even the Mets' chairman of board, M. Donald Grant, stopped by to tell Jim how pleased both he and owner Joan Payson were with the promotion. So Jim's first item of business was for us to decide when Mr. Met would make his next appearance. I was so relieved. I just knew that with the support of both Mets' management and ownership, Mr. Met could develop into a very successful and rewarding experience, not only for me but also for the franchise and, most importantly, the fans.

Pitcher Tug McGraw, *center,* was one of my best friends on
the team. Here he's reunited with a few of his old
teammates, including original Met Ed Kranepool, *back row,*
far left.

Most of our Sunday home games were doubleheaders. To entertain the fans between games, the Mets would often hire a renowned
marching band from the New York metropolitan area. Another doubleheader was scheduled for early June, and a very famous and successful band, the Hawthorne Caballeros, was scheduled to perform.
They were the defending New York State marching band champions.
Jim decided that Mr. Met would make an appearance with them. But
I was concerned about upstaging that accomplished ensemble and
possibly getting in their way, so I decided that I would play down Mr.
Met's role that day and just stay by the dugouts, wave to the fans, and
sign autographs. The bandmaster for the Hawthorne Caballeros,
however, had other plans. I greeted the band as they marched onto
the field, waving my arms excitedly and cheering them on as they
passed by. Suddenly, from out of nowhere, the bandmaster grabbed
my arm and dragged me out to the field with the rest of the troupe.

Now what do I do? As the band played and paraded up and down the field, I found myself instinctively dancing to the music. The more they played, the more I gyrated and strutted, leading the crowd in applause after each song. I was really getting into it, and at one point, during an upbeat Latin number, I almost lost my head … literally! I soon realized that my concerns about upstaging the Caballeros were completely unfounded. Both band members and fans alike were having a good time with it all. And the love affair between Mr. Met and the Shea Stadium faithful was beginning to blossom.

The initial Mr. Met appearances were very exciting and rewarding for me. But one thing did not change. The Mets still had a losing ball club. This was illustrated most dramatically at Shea Stadium on Father's Day, June 1964, in the first game of a Sunday doubleheader against the Philadelphia Phillies. We had a complete sellout in the stands that day, not unusual considering that it was a holiday doubleheader. But what was happening on the field was most unusual, even historic. The Phillies' hurler, the great Jim Bunning, was not only pitching a no-hitter, he was pitching a perfect game. It was now the sixth inning. I was getting ready to leave the press box for the clubhouse to get into my Mr. Met's costume. Looking back over my shoulder, I glanced up at the scoreboard and shook my head incredulously. Bunning had retired the first eighteen batters he faced and was still going strong.

By the time I arrived at the clubhouse and suited up, I realized that Bunning's domination against the Mets was moving the game along at an accelerated pace. It was already the top of the ninth inning, and the way Bunning was pitching, the game would be over any minute now.

I arrived at my station behind home plate just as the Mets were coming to bat in their half of the ninth. With the game just about lost, my thoughts turned immediately to Bunning and the fifty thousand Mets fans who were cheering him. I'm sure they wanted to witness a little piece of baseball history, so that years later they could say they were there. How could you blame them? But my concerns were less noble. What an act for Mr. Met to follow!

John Stephenson, a catcher for the Mets, struck out for the last out of the game. Bunning had pitched a no-hit, no-run, perfect game, and the crowd went wild. Mets fans called for Bunning to come out of the Phillies' dugout for a curtain call, something that was quite rare in those days. Many baseball players were genuinely concerned that such behavior would run the risk of showing up and alienating opposing players. And in the days when pitching high and tight to an opposing batter was allowed, even encouraged, getting the other team upset with you because of showboating was generally not a smart thing to do. But Bunning, sensing the historic nature of the moment, eventually came out of the Phillies' dugout to acknowledge the cheers of the fans. I went over to the Mets' dugout and joined in the applause. You could see on Bunning's face that he was enjoying the moment and the crowd's adulation. He must have enjoyed being in the limelight more than I thought, because after retiring from baseball, Bunning went on to pursue a career in politics as a United States senator.

The rest of the 1964 season was just as eventful. In addition to the All-Star Game held at Shea Stadium that year, Mr. Met went on to make appearances at the Old-Timers' Game and Banner Day, in addition to his regular Sunday doubleheader appearances. The Old-Timers' Game was quite a thrill for me. I was at home plate as each old-timer was introduced to the fans and had the opportunity to shake hands with many of my heroes. I admit, however, that it was a bit unwieldy, and some might say silly, meeting the former greats of the game with that huge baseball head resting precariously on my shoulders. But it was fun. Especially when Tom and Jim invited me to attend the old-timers' party afterwards—and I didn't even have to bring my head.

Chapter Five
Mr. Met Actually Wore Two More Heads

The 1964 Baseball season ended with the Mets once again finishing dead last in the National League, with a won-loss record of 53-109. The team, however, still managed to draw well over one million fans that year. Realizing that both the World's Fair across the street and the brand-new stadium probably contributed significantly to this achievement, the Mets' management believed improvements needed to be made on the field to maintain such lofty attendance figures.

The Yankees had lost the 1964 World Series to the St. Louis Cardinals, and both teams made major organizational changes during the off-season. In New York, Yogi Berra was fired by the Yankees as their manager and was replaced by Johnny Keane, the Cardinal skipper who had beaten the Yankees in the World Series only a few months earlier. And in St. Louis, Bing Devine resigned as general manager of the Cardinals and came over to the Mets as assistant to the president, George Weiss. Lost in all of these major organizational shuffles was my promotion out of the Mets' ticket department and into the team's promotion department as one of Tom Meany's assistants. However, unlike both Yogi Berra's and Bing Devine's announcements, there was no major press conference held that day.

Tom Meany and Jim Thomson got together with Bob Mandt and decided that my talents would best serve the organization as an assistant to Tom. Since Tom was responsible for both publicity and public relations, I was to assist him in the promotion department with John Geis as my counterpart in the publicity department. Prior to moving into Shea Stadium in 1964, the Mets didn't do much off-season promotion. But Tom began to change all that. It was now time for the players and coaches to go out into the community and meet the fans and thank them for their support. And so was born the Mets' Speakers Bureau Program. And Mr. Met was assigned to get it all started.

Shortly after the bureau's conception, Tom Meany had taken ill and was admitted into the hospital. A few times toward the end of the 1964 season, Tom had complained of not feeling too well. We lost Tom in the fall of 1964, and all of us who knew him and worked with him over the years, even to this day, think of him often. Herb Heft, an enthusiastic and energetic young public relations executive from the Minnesota Twins, was brought in to fill the void left by Tom's passing. It was not an easy task, but Herb was up to the challenge.

From the very beginning, Herb and I got along very well. I always believed this was because we both had the same goal: to make the Mets organization the most successful in baseball, both on and off the field. Herb was a strong believer in people. To illustrate this point, one night a group of us from the front office went bowling after work. Included in the evening's festivities were several staff members from other departments whom I didn't know. One such person, a young lady from the minor league department, asked Herb if I was the new guy working for him. Herb's reply was simple. "No, Dan is the new guy working *with* me." Little did I know at the time that Herb, John, and I, along with a capable young secretary by the name of Janice, would begin what would turn out to be a very innovative promotion and public relations department for the New York Mets. One such innovation was the Speakers Bureau Program.

Tug McGraw and I got together in the press box when he
was inducted into the Mets Hall of Fame. Tug was always the
life of the party. Sadly, he passed away in 2004 at age 59.

The Mets' Speakers Bureau Program started out modestly. There
were only four Mets players who resided in the New York metropolitan area during the off-season. Ed Kranepool, a young first baseman
who signed with the Mets right out of James Monroe High School in
the Bronx, lived near the ballpark in Queens. Ed was studying for his
broker's license on Wall Street and was very anxious to make appearances for the club, not only to pick up some extra cash but also to
make contacts for his future as a broker. He became one of the most
popular Mets and certainly one of the most cooperative players I had
the pleasure of working with over the years.

Another key member of the Mets' Speakers Bureau Program was
pitcher Tracy Stallard. Tracy, who gave up the record–breaking,
sixty-first home-run to Roger Maris while pitching for the Boston
Red Sox in the American League, was one of our veteran pitchers in
those early years and a team leader. In fact, he led the team in both
innings pitched and complete games in 1962. Since he lived in the

New York metropolitan area all year, Tracy made quite a few appearances for the Speakers Bureau during his stay with the Mets.

Larry Bearnarth, a young pitcher signed by the Mets out of St. John's University in New York City, was a Long Island resident and a high school teacher in the off-season. Larry was John Murphy's favorite young prospect when he was running the Mets' minor league system. And anyone who ever came in contact with Larry would understand immediately why John was so high on him. He had quiet leadership ability together with a dynamic personality. It was no surprise to any of us that Larry went on to become a pitching coach in the big leagues for both Montreal and Colorado. And I suspected that one day, he would make a great general manager for some major league franchise.

I enjoyed going on appearances with Larry. The vast majority were pleasant and uplifting experiences for Larry, the fans, and me. However, I will never forget one not-so-pleasant experience at a father-and-son that dinner Larry and I attended on Long Island. The gentleman who coordinated the event was very cooperative and friendly during our initial meetings. In fact, we had gotten along so well that he insisted that Larry and I come to his home before and after the appearance, to meet his family and just relax before going home. He was a prominent businessman on Long Island and, supposedly to enhance his stature in the community, bragged to several people that he was best of friends with Larry Bearnarth. Worse yet, he also boasted, falsely I might add, that he had gotten drunk with Larry the night of his Speakers Bureau appearance. When this got back to Larry, who lived at the time on Long Island, he was obviously very upset. After that incident, we were all much more careful about whom we were seen with and unfortunately kept our distance from many of the fans after an appearance was concluded.

Al Jackson, an original Met, was the team's most hard-luck pitcher. Al also lived on Long Island, with his wife and two little boys. He loved to make appearances on behalf of the Mets and always made an effort to talk to the young fans about staying in school and avoiding drugs and alcohol. Remember, this was the 1960s, when these problems were just starting to affect our nation's youth. Al had two little boys himself (who, by the way, loved Mr. Met) and took his Speakers Bureau appearances very seriously. However, when it was time to kick back and relax, you couldn't find a more fun guy to be around.

The last player to join the Mets Speakers Bureau Program in 1964 was Jack Fisher. Jack, who was the Opening Day pitcher at Shea Stadium for the Mets that year, came to the team from the Baltimore Orioles in 1963 and decided to live in New York City during the off-season. He expressed a genuine interest in making personal appearances locally to augment his income and to help promote his new team. And there certainly were enough appearances to go around. It wasn't exactly a living for players like Jack, but it did earn them a few extra dollars at a time in baseball history before the advent of free agency, skyrocketing player salaries, guaranteed contracts, and high-powered agents. And hopefully the Mets made a few new friends in the process. It must have helped, because as the Speakers Bureau Program expanded in subsequent years, attendance at Shea Stadium remained strong.

Shortstop Bud Harrelson, *right*, was another of my pals on the team. He is currently part owner of the Long Island Ducks minor league club. We were photographed in 2005 at a party.

One of the many other assignments that John Geis and I were responsible for was to coordinate the team's press conferences. Whenever there was a major trade by the club or a contract signing by one of our key players, a press conference was called to advise the media. Typically, this would include a luncheon in the Diamond Club at Shea Stadium and an appearance by the player himself, if he happened to be in town, so he could answer questions from the press, both print and broadcast. However, I vividly recall one exception to this policy that occurred in the winter of 1964.

The Mets' All-Star second baseman Ron Hunt had just lost out to Cincinnati Reds' second baseman Pete Rose as the National League's Rookie of the Year. Contract negotiations between Ron and team president George Weiss weren't going too smoothly. In the interim, John Murphy had been promoted to be Mr. Weiss' assistant. One of John's first responsibilities in his new assignment was to step into the contract negotiations with Ron on Mr. Weiss' behalf. Shortly thereafter, a settlement between Ron and the Mets was finalized. As was common in those days, Hunt had no agent representing his interests to Mets management. Contract negotiations, at a time before free agency, were strictly one on one, player versus management.

Ron was home in Missouri when he agreed to terms with the Mets, so a telephone hook-up was set up between Missouri and New York to allow Ron to answer questions from the media. At the conclusion of the telephone call, Herb Heft asked Ron if there was anything else he could do for him before ending the press conference. To my surprise, and in front of the entire New York City press corps, Ron asked Herb if "that guy who works in your office, Dan Reilly," was around. The phone line was still live for all in the room to hear when I got on to talk to Ron. All I could think of was maybe he wanted a few of his photos mailed to him in Missouri. That was a very common request from the players, since they usually responded to their own fan mail. Instead, Ron gave me the exact dates he was going to be in New York City to sign his contract and asked if I could arrange some Speakers Bureau appearances for him. Realizing that

Ron's request was for the purpose of supplementing his income, many in the press corps chuckled. Here was the National League All-Star second baseman, who had just agreed to terms with the Mets on a new contract, asking Dan Reilly, Mr. Met, to set up some personal appearances for him! Of course, I obliged.

Prior to this, I didn't know any of the local baseball writers that well. However, that press conference seemed to change all that. Once reporters like Dick Young from the *New York Daily News* and Jack Lang from the old *Long Island Press* realized my close relationship with the Met players, I quickly became pretty good friends with quite a few of them. In fact, Maury Allen, who chronicled the Ron Hunt press conference in the *New York Post* the very next day, remains to this day one of my closest friends.

Relief pitcher Ron Taylor joined the team in 1967 and was a key part of the 1969 championship year. He was another of my speakers and later became one of the most respected physicians in Canada.

Back in those days, baseball's Winter Meetings were held immediately after the World Series. This was a time of angst for the fans, as rumors of possible trades abounded, an element lost in today's meetings, since modern-day ballplayers' complicated and financially restrictive contracts tend to impede management's ability to make deals. For baseball front office personnel, it was also a time to address more mundane and practical matters, like the approval of next season's schedule. So while I was laying the foundation for the 1964 Speakers Bureau Program, Herb and John were beginning to formulate their promotional plans for the 1965 season. This would generally include next year's press guide and various promotions for the upcoming season. We would always laugh when people asked us what we did during the off-season, as if we shut down the entire organization until Opening Day of the following year. Nothing could be further from the truth, especially with George Weiss and his assistant, Bing Devine, running the organization.

Bing Devine was a solid baseball executive. His goal for the Mets was to develop young talent to replace the older veterans whom the organization had signed during the franchise's conception in 1962 and 1963. When Bing signed with the Mets in the winter of 1964, he also brought Eddie Stanky with him from the Cardinals organization to head up player development. Stanky was a familiar name to New York baseball fans, having played second base for many years with the Brooklyn Dodgers and New York Giants. Because of Stanky's aggressive play and never-give-up attitude, he was nicknamed "the Brat" by the New York media. In fact, there was still a little bad blood between Eddie and Phil Rizzuto regarding a hard slide Eddie made on Phil during the 1951 World Series between the Brooklyn Dodgers and New York Yankees.

Dodgers fans will never forget the day both Leo Durocher and Eddie Stanky left Brooklyn and went over to the hated New York Giants. Durocher, who managed the Brooklyn Dodgers from 1939 to 1948, was fired by the Dodgers during the 1948 season and hired shortly thereafter to manage the New York Giants. Stanky joined Leo as his third-base coach. In the famous "shot heard 'round the world," when Bobby Thomson hit the three-run homer for the New York Giants to beat the Brooklyn Dodgers for the 1951 National League pennant, you can see Eddie in the old film footage tackling Durocher halfway between third base and home plate, as Thomson rounded third base with the Giants' players waiting for him at home plate. If you weren't one of the many thousands of fans who claimed to be at the Polo Grounds that day, you most certainly heard Giants' announcer Russ Hodges' forever-famous radio call, "The Giants win the pennant! The Giants win the pennant!" … a cry that, to this day, still keeps many an old Brooklyn Dodgers fan up late at night wondering, "What if?"

So quite a few memories of baseball in "Little Old New York," both bitter and sweet, were evoked in the winter of 1964 when Bing Devine and Eddie Stanky joined the New York Mets organization. Another great New York baseball legend also joined the Mets that year, Yogi Berra. Yogi was a player-coach for the 1965 season. This infusion of knowledgeable baseball people like Devine, Stanky, Berra, and later Gil Hodges, and their ability to spot young talent and to teach baseball fundamentals were major steps the Mets were taking in 1964 to develop a much-improved and younger ball club as quickly as possible.

One of my more memorable weekends during the winter of 1964 was my first assignment as Herb Heft's assistant. Herb called me into his office one Friday afternoon and asked me if I had made any plans for Sunday. When I replied that I would be attending a party at Bob Mandt's home that afternoon, he seemed a little disappointed. I asked Herb what the problem was, and he told me that he needed a ride to LaGuardia Airport. It seemed that the Mets' management had just made a major deal and the player in question had to be picked up at the airport Sunday afternoon. However, it had to be done very discreetly, preferably by one of our staff. But due to his poor vision, Herb did not drive. I wanted to help in any way I could. Bob Mandt and I both lived close to the airport, so I assured Herb that it would not be a problem for me to slip away from the party to help him pick up our newest Met. Although I had a date for the party, I knew Bob would be willing to keep her company while I went off on my clandestine assignment.

I went home that Friday evening wondering who the newest "mystery Met" might be. Of course, I promised Bob Mandt that I would call him as soon as I found out. After all, he had agreed to keep my date company while I was off on my secret mission. I assumed this had to be a blockbuster deal, because a major press conference had already been scheduled for Monday. All kinds of rumors were floating about. The two most popular involved former New York Yankee personnel. Yogi had just been fired as their manager but had not yet come over to the Mets. Was Yogi about to join the Mets? Mel Allen, the legendary TV and radio announcer of the Yankees, had also been fired, and it was rumored he might be coming over to join the Mets broadcasting team. Mel was a very popular sports broadcaster in New York, and his departure from the Yankees was not received very well by their fans. So securing the services of such a popular New York sports icon would have been a major coup for the Mets franchise.

Sunday finally arrived. I dropped off my date at the party and drove out to LaGuardia Airport with Herb as planned. When we arrived at the airport, I noticed Herb checking the arrival time of a Northwest Airline flight from Milwaukee. It was then that he told me who the new mystery Met was: Warren Spahn, former Boston and Milwaukee Braves pitcher and future Hall of Famer. By the fall of 1964, Warren's best years were behind him, but in his prime, Warren Spahn was one of the greatest pitchers of all time. He was leaving the Braves after many years and was coming to the Mets to finish his illustrious career and, more importantly, to coach our young pitching staff.

What a thrill this was for me. I called Bob and gave him the good news. Bob found it hard to believe, since Warren was in the twilight of his career, while the Mets were in the process of building a much younger staff. However, once I told him that Warren would also be responsible for coaching our young pitching staff, Bob understood immediately why management went out and got him.

Less than an hour before the plane was scheduled to arrive, Joe Torre, then a catcher with the Milwaukee Braves, arrived at the terminal. In order to keep Warren out of sight until the next day's press conference, Herb's plan was to have Warren stay with Joe's brother, Frank Torre, at his home in Brooklyn rather than at a hotel in Manhattan. Joe and Frank would then take Warren out to Shea Stadium on Monday in time for the press conference. Herb's plan worked perfectly. When Warren arrived at the ballpark the next day, no one in the media had any idea why they were there or what was about to be announced. That was the first of many press conferences for me and, by far, my most memorable.

With all of the changes initiated in the 1964 off-season, things started to get even more exciting around Shea Stadium. Spring training was just around the corner, and reports of some young prospects signed by Bing Devine and Eddie Stanky abounded in the media. Springtime was fast approaching, and the fans were full of hope. With one more year of the World's Fair to help the team attract fans to the new ballpark and some promising young talent, the Mets and their fans braced themselves for the 1965 season.

Chapter Six
Speaking of the Mets

Just prior to spring training in 1965, Herb Heft received a major request from the owner of one of our minor league affiliates, the Auburn (New York) Mets in the New York–Penn League. These minor league affiliates, whether single-A or triple-A, were all very important to the Mets. They were the lifeline to the team's young prospects upon whom the organization's future was built, more so back in 1965 than today, since at that time there were few, if any, strong college baseball programs from which major league clubs could cull young talent. The minor league system was literally the only game in town. So the Mets always went out of their way to accommodate their minor league affiliates.

The Auburn Mets were planning a banquet to help support the ball club, and they needed as many big-name players as possible from the major league club to help boost attendance. This was a difficult request, since the banquet had been scheduled to be held about two weeks prior to the official opening of spring training. It was customary for many major league players to go to Florida early in order to get a head start on their workouts and training. Today, because of the amount of money generated by baseball, major league players usually work out all year round, even during the off-season, to keep themselves in the best physical shape possible. Good nutrition, vitamin supplements, proper rest, and scientific training methods are all part of today's year-round training regimen. However, this has not always been the case. Baseball players used to come to spring training looking to reverse several months of neglect and get back into shape. And if some were more neglectful than others, they usually wanted to begin their training before the manager and coaches arrived in camp. So the Mets really didn't have that many players available to send.

Thanks to Herb Heft and some great cooperation from within the organization, the problem was readily solved. Eddie Stanky, who at the time was traveling around the country scouting talent for the Mets, made himself available. Yogi Berra also agreed to attend, as did Mr. Devine and a few of us from the front office. Another addition to the group was a man who, in the years to follow, would become a very dear friend of mine, umpire Tom Gorman. Tom had a great reputation throughout baseball as one of the best storytellers and after-dinner speakers around. In addition to his duties as a National League umpire, Tom also worked as a spokesman for a large liquor distributor and made appearances on their behalf during the off-season. The Mets were very fortunate that Tom was available for this particular function. And I was honored to have been asked to attend with such an illustrious group of baseball people.

Bob Murphy joined the Mets at their beginning as a radio
and TV broadcaster. Here, he gives his induction speech at
the baseball Hall of Fame in Cooperstown.

We all flew on a private charter plane to Syracuse, New York. It was a memorable flight, to say the least. Evidently, Stanky and Yogi hadn't seen each other in quite awhile. Several of us were concerned that the 1951 World Series incident between Yogi's pal and former teammate, Phil Rizzuto, and Stanky would come up in conversation. Would there be bad blood between the two baseball greats? Would the normally brief flight between New York City and Syracuse be long, tense, and uncomfortable for us all? Thankfully, that was not the case. Both men were genuinely glad to see each other again. The incident was, in fact, brought up, but it was with such fondness and good humor that everyone on the flight enjoyed the discussion.

We were met at the airport by representatives of the Auburn ball club, who drove us to our motel, a short distance away. It was late afternoon when we checked into our rooms, so there was plenty of time to relax and get ready for the evening's festivities. As I was unpacking, I heard a tremendously loud voice calling from outside my room, "Reilly! Where is Reilly?" It was Tom Gorman. We had chatted on the plane, and I guess he could tell I was enjoying his stories about his interesting and humorous experiences in baseball. Tom had a couple of clients to see in the area and asked me if I wanted to tag along, just for an hour or so. Naturally, I checked with Herb, just in case he needed me for anything prior to the banquet. Herb gave me the OK, no questions asked. Actually, he was quite pleased that Tom and I had gotten along so well. I think Herb knew Tom would make a great addition to the Mets' Speakers Bureau Program. Well, Tom and I saw his clients and returned in plenty of time for the start of the banquet. Later that evening, Tom said he would call me when he was assigned a Mets' series so that we might get together. We also discussed his availability after the season for speaking engagements, since he knew that I was developing the Speakers Bureau Program. Tom was quite anxious to participate and became one of our more memorable speakers on the circuit.

Also attending the 1965 banquet in Auburn, as master of ceremonies, was one of the original voices of the Mets and one of my favorite

New York Mets of all time, announcer Bob Murphy. This was the first of what would be many public appearances I would make with Bob in the years to come. The organization didn't have much to be positive about in those early years. But Bob would talk about the Mets in such a positive way that you couldn't wait for the season to start. Like Tom Gorman, Bob too would subsequently become a very important and entertaining member of the Mets' Speakers Bureau Program.

The banquet itself went perfectly. Bob introduced each New York Met personality and, of course, Tom Gorman. I even got a chance to take a bow. I was introduced as Herb Heft's assistant and, for those who might have seen him on TV, Mr. Met himself. Surprisingly, several people in the crowd recognized Mr. Met, since some of the weekend Mets games were broadcast in Auburn via cable TV. That was very flattering for me personally and, more importantly, for the Mets. However, all of the speakers that day were great. Tom told his Casey Stengel and Leo Durocher stories. Yogi answered questions from the audience about his days as a New York Yankee. And Eddie Stanky not only talked about his days with the New York Giants and Brooklyn Dodgers but also mentioned his new duties as director of player development for the Mets. That night was the first time I heard the names of several promising young Mets prospects, including outfielders Cleon Jones and Ron Swoboda and relief pitcher Tug McGraw, all of whom would play key roles in the "miracle of '69." McGraw had pitched the previous year in Auburn. Not surprisingly, he was a big fan favorite there, and his name evoked a tremendous response from the crowd.

After dinner, we mingled with the fans while the more famous among us—Yogi, Stanky, Murphy, and others—posed for photos and signed autographs. All of us agreed that the dinner was an overwhelming success. We had successfully maintained the organization's strong relationship with one of its more successful minor league affiliates, and I was proud to be part of it all. And to think, it was only my first major banquet.

On the trip home, Eddie Stanky advised Herb Heft and me about his upcoming schedule and travel plans. Apparently, Eddie was planning on scouting several more young prospects around the country before spring training, with an eye towards possibly inviting them to camp that year for tryouts with the organization. Eddie was a tireless worker who took his responsibilities in player development for the Mets very seriously. When Bing Devine brought Eddie over with him from the Cardinals, the Mets were loaded with veteran players like Frank Thomas, Richie Ashburn, Gil Hodges, and Duke Snider, whose best years were behind them. But it was Bing's charge to Eddie to change all that. It was time to rebuild the Mets' organization into a young baseball franchise with a bright future. Few Mets fans today realize how instrumental both Bing Devine and Eddie Stanky were in that transformation. Thanks in large part to these two knowledgeable baseball men, the Mets went from being the most losing team in baseball history in its inaugural 1962 campaign all the way to winning the World Series in 1969.

Spring training in 1965 was well under way, and our job back in New York was to prepare for the upcoming baseball season. Once the season started, the organization's promotional efforts shifted away from public appearances and more towards various promotional events, like Banner Day and Old-Timers' Day. As usual, Mr. Met was scheduled to appear between games of Sunday doubleheaders, but several new appearances were added to the promotion schedule. Suddenly my season was starting to look quite busy.

One of the new promotion dates scheduled for Mr. Met in 1965 was Players' Family Day. This was always a very special day for everyone in the organization. It was a fun promotion in which the Mets played their sons and daughters before the regularly scheduled game. Immediately after the family game, Mrs. Payson, the team's principal owner and number one fan, would invite everyone connected with the game, except of course the players themselves, up to her private dining room for a party. Mrs. Payson always attended and actually ran the party herself. She gave out gifts to the children and made it a point to meet every child and to socialize with the players' wives. M. Donald Grant, chairman of the board and chief advisor to Mrs. Payson, often referred to all of us as the "Mets family." True, the team was owned and operated by affluent Wall-Street millionaires, but Mrs. Payson never let her money and social status get in the way of making all of us feel welcomed into her cherished Mets family. She was a truly great and loving woman.

Dan Reilly
(the original Mr. Met)

For several years, I hosted New York Waterway Shea Express, a boat ride for fans heading to games at Shea. It was fun to interact with the fans, reminiscing about the early Mets.

Another popular promotion for Mr. Met was Banner Day. For almost two hours, Mets fans would parade around Shea Stadium between games of a Sunday doubleheader, displaying their various Mets banners. Even though it was tough running around the ballpark in the summer heat for two hours with that big head resting heavily atop my shoulders, Banner Day was one of the organization's more successful promotions. And I always enjoyed being on the panel each year to help judge and select the winning banners. Yes, the 1965 season was a very busy one for me.

On the field, the team still finished last that year. However, the Mets brought up several of their young prospects to play with the major league club, and the future was starting to look brighter. Ron Swoboda, a young heavy-hitting outfielder from the Baltimore area, was considered a major prospect. So too was Frank "Tug" McGraw from California, the young left-handed pitcher the fans up in Auburn were so excited about. There was also a strong-armed, heavy-hitting outfield prospect that Bing Devine brought over from the Cardinals organization. His name was Johnny Lewis. Along with Swoboda in the outfield and a "young" veteran named Jim Hickman, the team was beginning to take on a whole new look. The 1965 season also saw the promotion of infield prospect Buddy Harrelson to the major league club. Buddy would eventually become an All-Star shortstop and one of the anchors of the 1969 championship team. The Mets had acquired veteran shortstop Roy McMillan the year before from the Milwaukee Braves. And as Warren Spahn had done previously with the team's young pitching staff, Roy took Buddy under his wing and taught him everything he knew about playing shortstop in the major leagues. In all, Mets fans were beginning to see the gradual transformation from an old veteran team to a young, promising, and dynamic baseball franchise.

In 1965 I was still a bachelor living in Queens, New York, with my pals from the airline industry. Ron Swoboda and his wife had rented a house in a beautiful little community called Whitestone, also in Queens and only about ten minutes from the ballpark. One day, Ron asked my friends and me if we would be interested in sharing the house with him and his wife. The Swobodas had not yet started their family, and the house was simply too large for just two people. They would live upstairs, and my friends and I would occupy the bottom half of the house, finished basement and all. It was all too good to be true! The owner of the house was an elderly woman who had recently been placed into a nursing home. Her son, a local priest, was looking for reputable tenants, since he was preoccupied with his mother's care and would not be able to spend much time keeping an eye on the house. The Swobodas were perfect tenants for the priest, since Ron and his wife Cecelia were respectable, family-oriented people who were planning to make New York their home all year long.

A later addition to our Whitestone family was Tug McGraw. Through a personal friend of mine, we arranged to get Tug into the Marine Corps Reserves in 1966 in order to fulfill his Vietnam-era military commitment. Personally, I think the Marine Corps training helped give Tug that extra confidence he needed to become a great relief pitcher and team leader. When Tug first started making Speakers Bureau appearances for the Mets, he was an instant success with the old-timers as well as our younger fans. He was confident and outgoing, no doubt the result, in large part, of his Marine Corps training.

Tug would frequently brag about how many great Irish bars there were back in his hometown of San Francisco and would often lament the paucity of such establishments in New York. Being of Irish descent myself, I felt it was my noble responsibility to set the young man straight. Not long afterwards, I introduced Tug to the Irish community in New York, and his love affair with the city began. We threw many a clandestine party in that house in Whitestone. I often thought about that priest from whom the Swobodas were renting and wondered whimsically what his reaction to those parties would have been. Needless to say, he was Irish.

The Speakers Bureau Program kept growing each year. But because the Mets' management was rebuilding the team in the mid-1960s, turnover of player personnel was widespread. Larry Bearnarth left the organization in 1967 and eventually retired as a player to become a coach with the Montreal Expos. Al Jackson also retired in 1966 and remained with the Mets organization as a minor league pitching coach, a position which he holds even to this day.

But there were several Mets players who were constants during those years. Ed Kranepool remained with the club for twelve years and was one of the organization's most reliable speakers. In fact, one year he and Ron Swoboda opened a restaurant in Huntington, Long Island, called "The Dugout" and made themselves available for many speaking engagements in order to promote their business. Jack Fisher, one of the Mets' more successful pitchers, was also very popular on the talk circuit. Another very special individual was shortstop Bud Harrelson. Buddy was very popular with the fans, both as a player and speaker. In 1967, he purchased a home on Long Island while he was negotiating his new contract with general manager Johnny Murphy. Upon finalizing his contract with the Mets, Buddy came directly into my office and asked me to book as many speaking engagements as I could for him. It seems that even with his new contract, Buddy was going to need a little help making those mortgage payments. Of course, I was only too glad to oblige.

Ron Taylor was another popular player for the Mets and a fan favorite on the talk circuit as well. Ron, one of the Mets' best relief pitchers of all time, not only had a degree in engineering, but also became a physician after his playing career was over. He lived in New York for a couple of winters back in the mid-1960s and truly enjoyed making appearances on behalf of the Mets. Ron and another relief pitcher whom the Mets received from the LA Dodgers, Larry Miller, always wanted details about their speaking engagements. For example, they wanted to know if the event was a father-and-son dinner or a Little League breakfast so that they could prepare their remarks accordingly. Larry sometimes gave a spiritual speech about the gift of playing ball and would also tell youngsters how lucky they were to have parents who cared about their future. I used to get many calls and thank-you letters from fans regarding the Mets players' participation in the Speakers Bureau Program, especially Larry and Ron. The Speakers Bureau Program was established to promote the ball club during the off-season and, at the same time, to establish a strong relationship between the players and fans. It worked so well that in 1965 the organization decided to develop a follow-up program, one that would be less promotional and oriented more towards community service. Affectionately dubbed the "Christmas Visits Program," it was an idea that I stumbled upon one Christmas during a speaking engagement with Al Jackson and Larry Bearnarth. I proposed to Met management that Mr. Met and selected Mets players visit children in several of the local hospitals during the Christmas holiday. I would perform as Mr. Met, and the players would hand out gifts and sign autographs.

Everyone in the organization, from management on down to the players, could not have been more enthusiastic about the proposal. But what would a hospital visit around Christmas time be without Santa Claus? Obviously we needed to find a Santa before initiating the program. Jim Thomson suggested Tom O'Brien, one of the best-liked guys in the organization. Tom was in charge of the press gate during the season. He was funny, very sharp, and certainly big enough to be Santa. In fact, Tom turned out to be the perfect Santa, especially because of his rapport with the kids.

I told Ed Kranepool and Jack Fisher about the program and, as family men themselves, they were both anxious to participate. We started out modestly that first year, visiting only a handful of hospitals. In subsequent years, we were able to expand the program to visit at least one hospital in each New York City borough as well as in Long Island, New Jersey, and Connecticut.

I'll never forget one visit to a local hospital in Flushing. Because of its location near Shea Stadium, the team used this facility for emergencies, most notably for on-and off-field injuries to the ballplayers. Jack Fisher was the Mets player participating that day. I appeared as Mr. Met, and several of our Diamond Club hostesses came along to help give out the gifts. The hospital always provided a place for us to change into our costumes, uniforms, and so forth, and this day was no exception. After visiting with the children, Jack was asked by the hospital staff if he would be kind enough to call on some of the older patients. Of course, Jack enthusiastically obliged. Tom, however, figuring we didn't need Santa for that audience, said that he would meet us later, downstairs in the area designated as our changing room.

After the visit with our older fans, we came back downstairs to change into our street clothes. However, Tom was nowhere to be found. Nobody knew where he was, not even the hospital staff. Suddenly I heard bursts of laughter coming from one of the nearby offices. There was a young girl sitting at a desk right outside the office door, so I asked her what was going on in there. She said it was the boardroom and there was a meeting currently in process. That sounded somewhat strange to me. A meeting of the hospital's board of directors with all that laughter? So we lightly knocked on the door and sheepishly opened it, not knowing what to expect on the other side. There was Tom, beard off, red coat unbuttoned, a big smile on his face, and a glass in his hand. Tom had taken over the hospital boardroom, and with his contagious personality and winning smile, helped those distinguished board members catch the Christmas spirit a little early that year! Tom passed away about two years into the program. You could not have met a nicer, more loveable guy than Tom O'Brien.

Another funny story involved Ron Swoboda and our 1966 Christmas visit to Bellevue Hospital in New York City. This time, after visiting the children, we were asked to visit the rehabilitation ward. Everyone there was pretty much taped from head to toe. As Ron was making the rounds, one patient, who had his head bandaged and was in a body cast up to his neck, motioned to Ron to come over. Ron, figuring the guy needed some cheering up, approached the young man directly. When he reached the guy's bed, Ron leaned over, ready to give him some words of comfort and encouragement. But before Ron could utter a single syllable, the young patient, mustering all of his strength and speaking in a barely audible voice, whispered inquisitively, "Why did you trade Charlie Smith?" Ron did all he could not to break out in laughter in front of this poor guy. Didn't he have much more to worry about than the Mets trading third baseman Charlie Smith? Such was the love affair in those days between New York fans and their beloved Mets.

We conducted these visits without seeking any publicity. It was our way of thanking the fans for their support and visiting those people, especially the children, who were unfortunate enough to be sick in a hospital during the holiday season. However, if the hospital chose to publicize our visit, especially to support their fund-raising efforts, that was up to them. Over the years, McGraw, Harrelson, and Berra also joined the hospital team. Many of the players made some new friends during their visits and kept in touch by visiting them on their off days. Remember, they were family men too.

Chapter Seven
Meet Me at the Fair

During the twenty-fifth anniversary reunion of the world-champion 1969 Mets, Tug McGraw asked me a trivia question that really stumped me. It was a two-part question. The first part was easy. Who was the first New York Mets pitcher to beat the great Hall of Fame pitcher Sandy Koufax of the LA Dodgers? It was obviously Tug himself back in 1965. The second part was a little more difficult. Where did we go to celebrate the victory? I was amazed that I could not recall that particular celebration. My memories of those years are so vivid, and Tug was one of my closest friends on the Mets. Well, after much thought and deliberation, Tug put me out of my misery. He gleefully reminded me, with an unmistakable twinkle in his eye, that we headed directly over to the Irish Pavilion at the World's Fair to celebrate with a few Irish coffees. Of course, that particular memory brought a smile to my face and a twinkle in my eye as well. But Tug and I both knew there was another story that went along with that particular incident, one that had gotten me into quite a bit of trouble with Jim Thomson.

I was in the press box at Shea Stadium just as Tug was about to get the last LA Dodger out in the ninth inning. Suddenly, Jim called me on the phone and suggested that I go down to the clubhouse after the game and bring Tug upstairs for a little celebration with the staff. When I arrived in the clubhouse, Tug had already started celebrating with a cold Rheingold. (Tug was always very loyal to all the Mets' sponsors, particularly Rheingold Beer.) Before I could mention the party upstairs, Tug suggested we run across the street to the fair for a quick one. Foolishly, I went along with his suggestion. Even though Tug was one of the more popular of the Mets players, I didn't expect so many people to recognize him at the fair. That spelled trouble for me. Many of the fans at the Irish Pavilion that day were all too eager to celebrate with Tug. Needless to say, we never made it back to the staff party. And boy, did I hear it from Thomson the next day. Even though it was only a small get-together, Tug and I realized that we should have attended Jim's celebration with the staff. I took the blame for that lapse in judgment. But even after twenty-five years, Tug still remembered appreciatively how I covered for him with Jim on that historic day in Mets history.

Original Mets photographer Dick Collins, *left*, talks with Tug McGraw following a game. Tug coined the phrase "Ya gotta believe" prior to meeting Cincinnati in the 1973 playoffs. The Mets beat the Reds, three games to two.

You can't talk about the early history of the New York Mets without discussing the 1964–65 World's Fair in Flushing Meadows Park. The Mets and the fair were right across the street from each other, literally only a five-minute walk door to door, and both will forever be historically linked. People from around the country and the world flocked to New York City in 1964–65 to see the World's Fair. Much like its predecessor in 1939 (also held in Flushing Meadows Park) and Disney's Epcot Center in Florida today, tourists came to the fair to learn about the past and get a glimpse of the future. Animatronics characters, so common in today's amusement parks, were introduced for the first time at the 1964–65 World's Fair. These included dinosaurs in primordial swamps and historic figures telling tales of past, present, and future deeds. In fact, General Electric's "Carousel of Progress," which was a popular exhibit at Disney's Epcot Center for over twenty-five years, was originally developed for the GE pavilion at the 1964–65 World's Fair in New York. Picture phones, the colonization of the moon and Mars, and the "City of the Future" were among the exhibits highlighted at the fair. And at a time when international travel was not quite as common and affordable as it is today, there were also exhibits and pavilions representing a myriad of countries from around the world. Many people were thus able to experience the sights, sounds, and foods of countries not readily accessible to them in their everyday lives. And many visitors to the fair would top the day off by attending a ballgame at Shea Stadium, arguably the premier, ultramodern sports stadium of its era, the prototype for other modern sporting arenas that would eventually be built around the country.

Because of the time pressures involved with our own Opening Day festivities and our hosting of the All-Star game that year at Shea Stadium, the 1964 baseball season was several months old before we finally made our first contact at the fair. His name was Jim Fitzgerald. Jim was in charge of security at the fair and had called our office seeking tickets for several World's Fair VIPs. Sensing the importance of this contact, I scheduled a luncheon appointment with Jim for the next day. What a great move that turned out to be for both of us. Jim had the authority to arrange special VIP visits for us to any of the exhibits and pavilions at the fair. In return, we could ensure that Jim's guests were given the VIP treatment at Shea, complete with complimentary tickets to the game, choice seating, their names on the scoreboard, and so forth.

Jim and I had an excellent working relationship. I suspect it was because we both grew up in the same neighborhood in New York City back in the 1950s and knew many of the same people. Both of us had also served in the Marine Corps. In fact, Jim was still very active in the Naval Reserves as a recruitment officer and was responsible for getting Tug McGraw into the Marine Reserves so Tug could fulfill his armed services commitment while continuing to play baseball.

The Mets made many new friends from around the world at the fair. It all started with a big media promotion in midsummer 1964 hosted by fair officials, called "New York Mets at the World's Fair Day." It was a most memorable day and very well organized. The entire team, including Casey Stengel, participated in the promotion, along with their families and several of our media people. The festivities included a motorcade around the fairgrounds, with stops at several of the more popular pavilions. Casey and his coaches were in the first car along with me, Mr. Met, followed closely by several cars containing the players and their families. Since the players wore only their Mets' warm-up jackets that day, it was actually easier to identify our section of the motorcade with Mr. Met and his big baseball head, than it was to identify the players trailing right behind us.

When we took a break for lunch, Dick Young, then a sports columnist for the *New York Daily News*, remarked to me that he couldn't help but notice how much enthusiasm Mr. Met was generating among the younger fans along the route of the motorcade. Casey, with his shiny grey hair and big floppy ears, was easy to identify, even without his uniform, and was always a fan favorite. But Mr. Met appeared to be the youngsters' choice that day. Perhaps this was because I was allowed on occasion to get out of the car to pose for pictures and sign autographs, something which the players were asked not to do. In their newspaper columns the next day, my old friends Dick Young, Maury Allen, and Jack Lang all wrote about the Mets' day at the fair and gave Mr. Met some very positive press in the process. It was most appreciated.

To help promote the World's Fair among Mets fans, several of the acts across the street were often invited to perform at Shea Stadium between games of doubleheaders. For example, the New Orleans Pavilion included a fun-filled replica of Bourbon Street, complete with strolling musicians and jazz bands. We would often go there after a night game to kick back and unwind. Not surprisingly, we asked many of their musicians to perform at Shea with Mr. Met, of course, who would dance along to the music with the best of them.

All of this cross-promotion between the Mets and the World's Fair made for some very interesting and, at times, funny stories. One such story involved the African Pavilion. We were invited there for lunch one day by the pavilion manager as a thank-you for entertaining several of their VIPs. This pavilion was one of the most beautiful in the fair. It had a lush, jungle-like setting with live animals, including monkeys and giraffes, roaming the grounds. The animals were all trained and were so docile that children could actually pet them. In the middle of the property, in a beautiful setting above the treetops, was a restaurant from which you could look down and see the animals roaming around the pavilion. Our host graciously joined us for lunch and, as was usually the case, the conversation soon turned to baseball and the New York Mets. I really started to get wrapped up in the discussion, talking optimistically about the Mets' future and the organization's young talent. Suddenly, Bob Mandt and several customers sitting adjacent to our table started laughing. I didn't really pay too much attention to them and continued on in earnest with my monologue about baseball and the Mets. Finally, I couldn't help but notice that everyone in the restaurant, including the servers and bus boys, was now laughing hysterically. Instinctively, I turned around to see what all the fuss was about. What I saw stopped me dead in my tracks. There, standing directly over my shoulder while I was busy talking, was this huge giraffe having a good old time chewing away at my salad! Everyone in the dining room, including yours truly, laughed heartily and enjoyed the moment. Whether on or off the field, the Mets were always good for a laugh or two.

Shea Stadium became almost like my home. I spent as many as sixteen to eighteen hours a day there when the team was in town. Opened in 1964, it will be torn down after the 2008 season to make way for a new park, but the memories will linger on.

The Mets' relationship with the World's Fair was truly very special. And because of my rapport with Jim Fitzgerald, I became the unofficial liaison between the Mets and the fair. If anyone wanted to go to a particular exhibit or restaurant, I would contact Jim, and he would handle the arrangements for us. It didn't take long before the entire National League learned about our special arrangement with the fair. I routinely received telephone calls from the players and officials of visiting clubs who wanted to take their families with them to New York City to see the fair. Of course, we did our best to help accommodate their requests. Typically, visiting players and their families would go to the fair or a particular pavilion or restaurant and receive VIP treatment. In return, the players would make themselves available for promotion or publicity shots. It was a match made in promotion heaven, both for the World's Fair and their officials as well as the ballplayers, club executives, and their families. More importantly, however, the sincere courtesies extended by fair officials to all of us in the baseball community were deeply appreciated.

Of course, all relationships have their occasional disappointments. And the Mets' relationship with the World's Fair was no exception. One disappointment involved a Sunday doubleheader against the Houston Astros, our National League expansion rivals. As usual, I checked well in advance with my contacts at the fair to scout entertainment for the doubleheader. To my surprise and delight, I discovered that the University of Southern California marching band (the USC Trojans) was performing at the fair that Saturday evening. When approached about staying in New York City an extra day to perform at Shea Stadium, the members of the band expressed a genuine interest and enthusiastically accepted our invitation. They were originally scheduled to fly back to California Sunday afternoon but changed their departure to Sunday evening to accommodate our request. Every detail had been finalized, including our usual advanced publicity.

However, when Sunday morning came, so did the rains. It was raining pretty hard when I arrived at the ballpark at 10 a.m. and it just wouldn't let up. Houston was in the Western Division of the National League, and the team would only be back in town one more time. Every effort was going to be made to try and play the doubleheader, or at least one of the games, so we called the band at their hotel in Manhattan and told them to come out to the stadium. When they finally arrived at Shea and got off the bus in their classic Trojan uniforms, it still didn't look very promising. It was raining steadily, with no end in sight. Eventually, the doubleheader was canceled and I had to be the one to give the kids the bad news. I waved good-bye as they drove off to the airport to catch their flight back to California. I still remember the disappointment etched on all of those young faces. I guess being from southern California, a rainout was a very difficult concept for them to accept. At least that's what several native Californians later told me.

By 1965, the relationship between the Mets and the World's Fair had cemented quite strongly. In fact, the Mets promoted their annual Old-Timers' Day game that year by scheduling corresponding festivities at the fair. World's Fair officials agreed to host a weekend-long celebration at the fair, concurrent with the game itself. All of the Mets old-timers arrived in New York City a day early so that they could participate in the weekend's promotional events. The Old-Timers' Game itself was held on Saturday afternoon, with the weekend's festivities beginning on Friday and ending on Sunday. One of my responsibilities that weekend was to take the charter bus into Manhattan to pick up the old-timers at their hotel and to shuttle them and their families to and from the various weekend events. As a baseball fan myself, it was truly an honor to meet so many of my childhood heroes and their families. Unquestionably, that weekend was the highlight of the 1965 baseball season for me.

When they closed the World's Fair in the fall of 1965, Bob Mandt, myself, and several of our co-workers were probably the last people to leave the fair grounds in the wee hours of the morning. Sadly, the good times and acquaintances that had sprung from our special relationship with the fair faded into history that night. Never again would we see our friends from across the street. Never again would we be able to say to one another with a twinkle in our eye and a spring in our step, "Meet me at the Fair!"

Chapter Eight
After Casey and the Fair—Now What?

The 1965 season was rolling along, and yet the Mets still couldn't find that winning combination. Warren Spahn pitched for the team, hoping that his experience and professionalism would rub off on some of the younger pitchers. Soon afterwards, Yogi retired from playing and became a coach for the Mets. A few promising young players like Swoboda, Kranepool, and McGraw were coming along. But the organization knew it had a long row to hoe because its pitching was still very weak.

Bing Devine and Eddie Stanky were constantly on the road scouting young talent, especially pitching. Many of us in the Mets organization were hoping that some of the magic that both gentlemen had worked while they were with the Cardinals would somehow come our way as well. Then came that infamous date in Mets' history ... Saturday, July 24, 1965. The team was celebrating Casey Stengel's seventy-fifth birthday with a cake and ceremony at home plate at Shea Stadium. Of course, Mr. Met was by Casey's side, cheering on the fans and wishing him all the best. Later that day, it was off to Toots Shor's Restaurant in midtown Manhattan for the real party.

The gathering for Casey's birthday party read like a who's who in New York City baseball. Casey's old pals from the Yankees, including Mantle, Ford, Berra, and Rizzuto, were all there, as were several local celebrities and most of the newspaper reporters who covered the Mets. It was a real collection of serious partygoers, and a splendid time was had by all. Or almost all. Towards the end of the evening, several of us heard some commotion coming from the men's room. When we arrived on the scene, we found Casey on the floor. It seemed that he had slipped and hurt his hip. Joe DeGregorio, the organization's comptroller, agreed to take Casey home in his car. However, Casey was in so much pain that Joe later decided to take him to Roosevelt Hospital instead. Casey's injury turned out to be much more serious than anyone had originally thought; it was a fractured hip, which naturally would confine him to the hospital for an extended period of time.

The next day, at a hastily called press conference, the team announced that coach Wes Westrum would fill in for Casey as interim manager. At the time, no one in the organization had any idea how serious Casey's injury really was. All kinds of rumors were flying around about the cause of his accident, including everyone's favorite, which had Casey falling off a barstool at Toots Shor's. Only a few of us who were there that night knew the true story, but we felt that Casey breaking his hip on the bathroom floor at Toots Shor's was not a very flattering public image for the old man. We didn't want Casey's fans to view this grand old man of baseball, a revered sports legend of his day, in such a potentially embarrassing light. So it was agreed by all that we would keep this little story to ourselves, for Casey's sake.

"CASEY'S LAST FAREWELL"
SHEA STADIUM   AUGUST 1965

Casey Stengel retired as the Mets' manager in 1965. Some
still call him the original Mr. Met because he was so closely
associated with the team in the public mind.

After the press conference, a large crowd of media people waited outside Wes Westrum's office for some news about Casey's condition. One of the reporters that day was the former New York Football Giants great, Frank Gifford. I had held season tickets to the Football Giants' games for a few years, going back to my airline days, and Gifford was one of my favorite players. Frank had recently retired and was just starting his new career as a reporter for CBS Channel 2 Sports. Frank looked a little perplexed that day, so I went over and asked him if I could be of any help. Apparently he was under a very tight deadline and wanted to get an interview with Wes Westrum, the Mets' new manager. I was always happy and willing to help a young person starting out in a new career, so I went to Wes' office and told him of Frank's dilemma. Wes, a knowledgeable baseball man and all-around nice guy himself, said he would take care of it. He and the Mets could always use the publicity. So that evening, there was Wes being interviewed on the evening news by Frank. Always glad to help, Frank!

Helping me arrange Frank's interview with Wes that day was Harold Weisman, the Mets' new public relations director. With all of the media attention generated by both Shea Stadium's inauguration and the 1964–65 World's Fair, Herb Heft's duties as both promotion and public relations director had become too much for one person to handle effectively. So the Mets hired Harold away from the old *Daily Mirror* newspaper, which has since gone out of business. The Mets' publicity efforts were so extensive that Harold, too, needed an assistant. So he hired a young man by the name of Matt Winnick. Matt had a very strong statistical background and was experienced in media relations, having helped most of the reporters who covered the Mets. Matt would later go on to enjoy a long and successful career with the Mets, and today he works in the NBA Commissioner's office.

While with the Mets, Matt and I became very good friends and shared many a story together. One such tale involved a major banquet in Newark, New Jersey. It was the Newark Boys' Club Dinner; the Mets' new general manager, Bing Devine, had been invited, along with the team's star first baseman, Ed Kranepool. As usual, I did the driving and Matt sat next to me in the front seat. In the back were Bing and Ed. Around this time, Ed was having contract problems with the club, and spring training was only a few weeks away. Nonetheless, both Ed and Bing appeared to be in good spirits that evening.

The evening went very well. The fans had a great time meeting Kranepool and hearing Devine talk proudly about the Mets' future. The enthusiasm and goodwill generated among the Mets' faithful that night, both young and old, was high. On the way home from the affair, Bing and Ed once again were sitting in the back seat, but now they were talking seriously about God knows what. I was too busy driving to listen to their conversation. Nor did I care. And Matt, who was sitting beside me trying to get some shut-eye, paid no attention as well. We dropped Bing off at the Hilton Hotel in Manhattan where he was staying and then started back to Shea Stadium, where Kranepool had parked his car. As soon as we dropped off Bing at the hotel, Ed looked at us from the backseat and said, with a huge sigh of relief, "Well, that's taken care of!" We had no idea what he was talking about. Within minutes, Ed told us that he and Bing had just reached an agreement on his contract and that it would be announced the next day at a press conference. All the way back to New York, they were sitting in the back seat of the car talking contract, literally in front of Matt and me, and we had no idea what was going on.

With today's player representatives and agents, financially lucrative long-term contracts, and free agency, I doubt very much that baseball will ever again see such direct, hands-on negotiations between a player and management. For better or worse, those days are gone forever. But back in the mid-1960s, face-to-face negotiations between a player and management were the norm. There were no agents. In fact, most, if not all, general managers would refuse to negotiate with anyone other than the ballplayer himself, and animosity sometimes developed on both sides. However, Bing's direct, honest, and genuinely sincere style was appreciated and respected by the players themselves and his peers in other major league ball clubs—a style that would also be adopted by his successor, Johnny Murphy.

Bing took over as general manager of the Mets after George Weiss retired in 1967. He immediately initiated several major changes in the baseball end of the operations, particularly the organization's scouting and minor league operations. Bing also accelerated the policy of bringing in veteran ballplayers to be tutors and mentors for the team's promising young prospects. One such veteran was the great defensive shortstop, Roy McMillan, who was then coming to the end of an illustrious baseball career. Roy, who had joined the club in 1964 after playing for the Milwaukee Braves, was assigned to work with the Mets' promising young shortstop, Bud Harrelson. It must have worked, because Bud went on to become one of the best shortstops in Mets' history.

Buddy made it to the major leagues despite some roadblocks along the way. During the Mets' 1965 Old-Timers' Day promotion at the World's Fair, I had an interesting discussion with a former Brooklyn Dodgers great of the 1930s and '40s, first baseman Dolph Camilli. Dolph, who was then the chief West Coast scout for the New York Yankees, talked glowingly about a young shortstop he had scouted in San Francisco. He really loved the kid's ability and style and thought he was a bona fide major league prospect. However, Dolph had been voted down by the Yankee brass, who thought the kid was too small to play in the major leagues. That young prospect who, if Dolph had his way, would have played shortstop at Yankee Stadium rather than Shea Stadium, was Bud Harrelson. I listened incredulously as Dolph told his story. All I kept thinking to myself was, didn't they say the same thing about one of the great Yankee shortstops of all time, Phil Rizzuto?

Yogi Berra played briefly for the Mets in 1965. He then
retired and became first-base coach and batting instructor
under the great manager Gil Hodges. He himself later
became manager, staying with the team through 1975.

As Bing Devine was rebuilding the Mets' front office in 1967, many of us in the organization began to get a little nervous. Bing was hiring additional personnel from the St. Louis Cardinals franchise, and many of us in Flushing were getting increasingly anxious about our jobs. As in most industries, this sort of thing happens in professional sports; whenever a new chief executive comes into an organization, he (or she) wants to bring in his own staff. One day, shortly after being named general manager, Bing called a staff meeting. Interestingly, everyone attended except the baseball and talent end of the organization. The ticket department, promotions and public relations, accounting, the ladies who handled fan mail, and other special services were all present. Rumors of all types, mostly negative, had run rampant throughout the organization for days. But when Bing took the floor, he got right to the point. The Mets, with their strong attendance and uncanny popularity throughout the country, were the talk and envy of baseball. Considering the team's perpetually losing record, Bing could only attribute that success to the abilities and efforts of all of us in the room. And he wanted to congratulate each of us personally. Bing went on to tell us that his goal was to build a winning ball club on the field to match our success off the field.

In my opinion, 1967 was a turning point for the Mets organization. Casey had retired. (Casey subsequently passed away in 1975.) The World's Fair was over. Several veterans were being signed by the club, and the franchise's minor league system was beginning to produce some talented young prospects. Bing was starting to make good on his promise to improve the ball club on the field. One of the veteran players Bing brought over to the Mets was Ken Boyer. Ken came to the Mets from Bing's old organization, the St. Louis Cardinals, where he excelled for fifteen years. He was a bona fide All-Star, a club leader, and one of the premier baseball players of his era. Ken set a great example for the Mets' younger players both on and off the field. Some may remember that Ken was the older brother of Clete Boyer of New York Yankees fame. Clete was also a great third baseman. But while Clete excelled on the field with his glove, Ken was an above-average defensive third baseman in his own right, who hit for power and average.

Ken and Clete Boyer were not the only connection between the Mets and Yankees in the late 1960s. For a time, there was a group of Yankees and Mets players all living together in Queens. Clete had retired and become a coach for the Yankees, while Ken was playing for the Mets. Both brothers shared an apartment not far from Shea Stadium. Also living in that apartment with the Boyer brothers was a relief pitcher by the name of Hal Reniff. During his major league career, Hal had pitched for both the Yankees and Mets. To complete this group, there was a little known outfielder—just acquired from the Kansas City Athletics by the Yankees—named Roger Maris. Roger stayed at the apartment at the beginning of the 1966 season because his family was still in Kansas City waiting for the school year to be completed.

Ken, Clete, and several other players used to frequent a small res-taurant near their apartment where I had also been know to stop in on occasion. There was a very talented piano player in the restaurant at the time, and I had the reputation of always being willing to join in with him to belt out a song or two. One night, I was singing gleefully at the piano, having no idea that Ken and a few other ballplayers were sitting in the back of the restaurant, taking it all in. Boy, did I hear about it the next day in the clubhouse! From that day on, Ken would good-naturedly get on me about my singing. I guess my talent for song was not as good as I thought it was. I still cannot figure out why Ken Boyer is not in the Hall of Fame. But that is a subject for another time.

Another veteran who was brought in by Bing Devine to set an example for the Mets' young prospects was Eddie Bressoud, an infielder from the Boston Red Sox. Ed was a high school teacher in the off-season back in California. He had excellent work habits and was always one of the first players on the field for batting practice; he could always be seen discussing baseball and opposing players with the Mets' young prospects. Ed was definitely managerial material, maybe even capable of aspiring someday to become the general man-ager of a major league club. But teaching was always Ed's first love, I guess.

When the Mets started bringing up their younger players in 1965, it was truly something to behold. There were outfielders Ron Swo-boda and Cleon Jones, shortstop Buddy Harrelson, first baseman Ed Kranepool, and pitchers Tug McGraw, Jerry Koosman, and Gary Gentry. To fill the team's need for an everyday catcher, Bing Devine traded for Jerry Grote from the Houston Astros.

Nolan Ryan deserves special mention. When Nolan came up to the Mets from their farm system in 1968, we were all amazed by his incredible fastball, which was already the talk of the National League. I will never forget the afternoon Nolan came in to relieve against the Pittsburgh Pirates and faced none other than Roberto Clemente. Some say Clemente may have been one of the greatest players of all time. Such recognition was probably hindered by the terrible plane crash that took Clemente's life in the prime of his career while he was attempting to deliver hurricane relief supplies to his native Puerto Rico. Nolan Ryan struck out Clemente on three pitches that day, a feat unheard of at the time. Clemente rarely struck out, let alone on only three pitches. I can still see Clemente, walking back to the dugout while staring coldly out at the mound, wondering just who that was out there. That was the beginning of Nolan's memorable career and I was so proud to see it from the start.

Jerry Koosman almost won Rookie of the Year in 1968; he became another key addition to what was to become a dominating pitching staff. This brings me to the player who, in my opinion, was the greatest Mets pitcher ever, and surely one of the great pitchers of all time, Hall of Famer Tom Seaver. Tom came to the Mets in 1967 out of the University of Southern California and was an instant success, both on and off the field. When Tom first joined the club, Matt Winnick brought him to visit the various offices in the organization. He seemed sincerely interested in what the different functions were in the various departments. And you could sense immediately that he had a solid appreciation for public relations based on his schooling at Southern California. I personally enjoyed working with Tom because he was very cooperative and fun to be around. But his accomplishments on the field are what set Tom apart from everyone else who ever wore a Mets uniform. For example, Tom was Rookie of the Year in 1967, a two-time Cy Young Award winner (1973 and 1975), and had 311 major league career victories.

These young men were all a joy to work with. They realized that we all were responsible for maintaining the Mets' popular image with the fans, and they all seemed to want to contribute. Just as important, they all wanted to be part of a winning team and organization. It was only going to be a matter of time.

But more than just baseball was beginning to take hold in Flushing, Queens, in the era that followed Casey Stengel and the World's Fair. The upstart American Football League's New York Jets were our cotenants at Shea Stadium. Formerly known as the New York Titans, the Jets also played at the old Polo Grounds beginning in 1962 during the early days of the American Football League. The AFL would subsequently merge with the NFL, as the direct result of the Jets winning Superbowl III in 1969 against the heavily favored Baltimore Colts. (The ill-fated city of Baltimore lost both the World Series and the Super Bowl in 1969 to young, upstart teams from New York!) Many a book has chronicled the Jets' success throughout the years. But to my knowledge, very little has been written about the great working relationship that existed between the Mets and Jets organizations, particularly with respect to their front office personnel.

Before the Jets built their beautiful training complex at Hofstra University on Long Island, both teams trained and played their home games at Shea Stadium. Shea, after all, was the first of a new generation of modern, all-purpose stadiums designed for both baseball and football. The lower field box seats at Shea sat atop giant casters, which allowed the seats to be rolled out at an angle parallel to the football field for better viewing. During baseball season, the lower field box seats were rolled back after each football game to conform to the stadium's baseball configuration. Nonetheless, it was very difficult for the Jets at times, since they had to work their schedule around the Mets and their home games.

The Jets were owned by Sonny Werblin, a legend in the world of entertainment and sports. The first time I met Mr. Werblin was when Bob Mandt was showing him around the Mets' ticket department. I could tell immediately that he was a hands-on type of owner and wanted to be involved in every aspect of the operation. Another impression I had of Mr. Werblin was that if you worked for him, you would be well taken care of, provided you gave your very best. Over the years, I learned from many of my friends working for the Jets that this was in fact the case.

The Jets sometimes practiced at Shea Stadium, so we became friendly with most of them. Late one afternoon during a week when the Mets were out of town, the Jets were practicing at the stadium.

Those of us in the Mets' front office had finished our day's work and headed down the street to our favorite little Italian restaurant for dinner and a couple of drinks. When we arrived at the restaurant, about ten huge guys were sitting at the bar. We immediately recognized them as Jets players. Shortly after we all acknowledged each other, drinks were sent our way by none other than the legendary quarterback for the New York Jets, Joe Namath. Well, that made my day. Namath was such a huge figure in New York sports in the 1960s that I couldn't believe he would take the time to make such a nice gesture. It was a pleasure to be in the company of all those guys, Namath included.

Chapter Nine
Now a Word
from Our Sponsors

Every year when September came around and the season was winding down, those of us in the Mets' front office were always asked the same question: "What do you guys do in the off-season?" I would usually explain how the preliminary schedule for the following baseball season is presented to all the ball clubs in the fall and finalized at the Winter Meetings in November. That's when everyone agrees on the number of doubleheaders and night games, based on guidelines established in the labor agreement between the major leagues and the players. For example, teams would try to avoid night games on getaway days, when one or both teams have to travel to the next city on their schedule.

We always tried to keep the Judge, Bill Gibson, out of these discussions, because you never knew what would come out of this guy's mouth. I remember him once trying to make a case that all of us who worked in the front office should live near Shea Stadium because, as he said, "They're ready to put a dome on Shea's roof, and we all have be here to supervise." This is a true story … that is, the story is true, not the part about the dome!

These "intellectual discussions" usually took place at one of our favorite establishments, Breslin's, which was located right by Shea Stadium. Breslin himself (no relation to the famous writer, Jimmy

Breslin) held season tickets for the Mets and always came up to the Diamond Club after each ballgame to share a drink or two with his friends in the front office. We all became like family and would sometimes go to his place after leaving the Diamond Club. With the long hours we would put in at Shea, all of us really looked forward to relaxing after work with our friends down the block at Breslin's.

The Mets' Speakers Bureau Program also took up a lot of my time during the off-season. The requests for speakers generally built up during the summer months. And it was then that I would inquire about players' availability for appearances during the coming off-season. As the program grew, my stable of speakers would change from year to year, generally for the better.

Two such players were pitcher Ron Taylor and catcher Duffy Dyer. Talk about cooperation. These two guys really enjoyed making appearances on behalf of the organization (not that the other players didn't) and meeting the young Mets fans. Ron talked to the youngsters about the value of staying in school and getting an education. He was definitely the right guy to deliver that message, for in addition to playing major league baseball, Ron was an electrical engineer and was also studying to be a physician. Duffy also loved to make appearances and was an excellent speaker. He was particularly fond of attending our special Christmas visits.

Lindsey Nelson, Bob Murphy, and Ralph Kiner, the Mets'
original broadcasters, went on to become one of the
longest-running broadcasting teams in professional sports
history. They are wearing patches for Rheingold Beer, one
of the team's first sponsors.

In addition to our usual requests for public speaking engagements
during the off-season, we also worked with our radio and television
sponsors. Rheingold Beer was the flagship sponsor of the Mets. They
held their major sales meetings and seminars at Shea Stadium during
the season and even requested that certain Mets players be available to
speak at various corporate functions and promotions.

There was one particular promotion which the Mets and Rheingold Beer worked together on every February, just before the start of
spring training, that was always a lot of fun. It was the Sport and
Travel Show held at the New York Coliseum near Central Park in
Manhattan. The show ran for ten days and consisted primarily of

hunting and fishing exhibits. We shared a booth with Rheingold Beer, and the show was always great exposure for both organizations. It also was an excellent opportunity for those of us with the Mets to hand out our upcoming season's schedule and possibly sell some season tickets. One of Rheingold's sales people and I would usually coordinate that effort, assisted by several of our Diamond Club ladies. The young ladies would hand out schedules that were printed by Rheingold and that prominently displayed Rheingold's name and promotional logo. And we would always be sure to have a celebrity appear at the booth during prime-time hours to attract traffic. In most cases, this would usually be a Mets player.

We were very lucky one year to have two popular New York Mets celebrities participate in this promotion. Ron Hunt was in New York on personal business before going to Florida for spring training and made himself available to attend the show. So too was Eddie Stanky, just off a long scouting assignment for the general manager, Bing Devine. What a pleasure it was working with those two gentlemen. Ron and Eddie were so cooperative. They alternated the days of their appearances at the booth, and it worked out great, both for us and the fans.

I will never forget the day Eddie Stanky was with us at the booth and decided to walk around the Coliseum to take a break and look at the various exhibits. I knew Eddie was from Alabama but did not realize that he was an avid hunter. Ed came back to our booth and asked me if I had gotten to know any of the other exhibitors. I told him I knew a few of the people from just walking around, but that I really had no interest in any of the hunting or fishing exhibits. He mentioned that he saw a beautiful hunting rifle that he was interested in for his son back home. So later I went over to the man who was managing the exhibit and told him that Eddie Stanky was interested in one of his rifles. He was overwhelmed. Eddie always kept a very low profile and hadn't told the guy who he was. The manager asked me if Ed would pose for a picture at his exhibit, and he, in turn, would give him the rifle. This would be just a straight promotional deal, with no conflict of interest at all. Eddie was more than happy to cooperate, and the rifle was later mailed to his son in Alabama.

While Eddie was with us at the booth, he also found out that Ted Williams, the greatest hitter of all time, was visiting a nearby fishing exhibit. So he asked me if I would like to meet Ted. "What do you think? I suppose I could squeeze Teddy Baseball into my busy schedule," I responded sarcastically. So Eddie brought me over to meet Ted and even told him how appreciative he was of what I had done for him regarding the rifle. Ted shook my hand and thanked me for doing a special favor for a dear friend of his. It seems that Stanky and Williams had been old friends for years, not only through baseball, but also because of their mutual love of the outdoors.

What a great day that was for me. And to top it all off, I later received a phone call from Eddie telling me that he had told Bing Devine about the great job I was doing at the show. He then suggested that I invite Bing over to the Coliseum to see the operations for himself. When Bing arrived, he was impressed not only with the show but also with our entire off-season promotion schedule. He was very appreciative of our efforts and agreed that no other organization in baseball worked as hard in the off-season as the Mets' front office personnel.

Our promotions would not have been successful without the cooperation of our sponsors. Rheingold worked with us all year long, printing new schedules and brochures and participating with the Mets and our players on outside promotions. And then there was Bordens, known for their line of quality dairy products, including milk and ice cream. Everyone who grew up in New York City back then remembers Elsie the Cow, the smiling, friendly caricature that appeared on all of their products' packaging and promotions. Bordens even had an Elsie the Cow balloon each year in the famous Macy's Thanksgiving Day Parade in New York City. As most of you I'm sure know, those balloons are carried mostly by Macy employees and fly well above the crowd of spectators as the parade proceeds down Broadway towards Macy's at Herald Square. Elsie would join cartoon characters like Popeye the Sailor, Superman, Bullwinkle, and the list goes on. The Macy's parade is a true holiday tradition in New York and around the country.

I was at my desk one afternoon in early November 1966 when our secretary, Fran Hanihan, told me that Jim Thomson would like to see me in his office right away. What could it be about? All the Mets ballplayers had been making their scheduled appearances for the Speakers Bureau Program. So I had no clue why Jim might want to see me. Well, it seems that he just had lunch with several of Bordens' executives and was told how pleased they were with their relationship with the Mets. And it certainly didn't hurt my career to have my name brought up several times by the Bordens group during that luncheon.

The Bordens people also told Jim that Elsie would make her last appearance in the Macy's Thanksgiving Day Parade that year, after over twenty years of faithful service to the company. Jim, the born promoter that he was, thought it would be a great idea if the Mets could help Bordens celebrate this historic occasion. So, of course, he volunteered Mr. Met's services. It was a great idea. Just think of the national exposure the Mets would get as our group, led by Mr. Met, marched with the Elsie balloon on national television!

Everyone in the organization was really excited both about helping Bordens and seeing Mr. Met march in the parade. Jim told his family and friends on Long Island to watch the parade on television; the rest of the organization wished me well. Everyone couldn't wait to see Mr. Met on national TV. But there was one little surprise, at least for me. Jim wanted Mr. Met to ride a bicycle, so that he could more readily say hello to the children who would be lined up on either side of Broadway along the parade route. It sounded like a good idea, so we included the bicycle in our parade plans.

We assembled that Thanksgiving morning at 8:30 a.m. at West Eighty-sixth Street near Central Park in Manhattan. As you may know, the parade route extends all the way down Broadway and ends at Macy's on Thirty-fourth Street at Herald Square. That's nearly three miles, on a bicycle, no less. But that was just the beginning of my problems. When developing our plans for the parade, we had forgotten about the head! The Mr. Met head could not be removed, especially in front of the parade spectators and children. With the head's weight and limited peripheral vision, navigating side to side to say hello to the kids along the parade route was virtually impossible. Moreover, the winds that day blew so hard against my huge head that it was a miracle I was even able to stay on my bicycle! I did get a chance to take a breather whenever the parade halted. But I know what it must have looked like. To the casual observer, it had to look as if Mr. Met may have indulged in a few too many spirits that Thanksgiving holiday morning!

We finally arrived at the reviewing stand, where the NBC-TV crew was broadcasting the parade to millions of viewers nationwide. Finally, here was Mr. Met's chance to be on national television. All of the tedious maneuvering with that huge head and my tiring fight against those blustery winds was about to pay off. The time was now! Once we had passed the reviewing stand, I was exhausted. I was also very proud of myself and my colleagues for weathering the storm and helping the Mets get some valuable national TV exposure. When I got home, however, I received the most disappointing news. After all that work and struggle, no one saw Mr. Met on TV that Thanksgiving morning.

The next day, Jim told me he had seen Elsie the Cow in the background, a few blocks away, and *might* have caught a brief glimpse of Mr. Met struggling to stay on his bicycle off in the distance. But that was it. Apparently, NBC cut away to a commercial just as we arrived at the reviewing stand. Just our luck! Indeed, it seemed in those days that the Mets couldn't even catch a break at Macy's Thanksgiving Day parade.

Of course, the Bordens people were still very pleased with our participation in the parade. And our relationship with that beloved and valued sponsor solidified even further that day. Their promotions with the Mets during the baseball season were always very successful. For example, on special promotion dates, all fans could get a free general admission ticket to the game just by presenting ten coupons from any Bordens product at a designated stadium gate. This was a very popular promotion, especially among young fans who could not afford to purchase reserved seat tickets. However, it did become a bit unwieldy to manage during some of the more popular game dates, like a Friday night game against one of our better opponents. But it was well worth it. I'm sure that singular fan-friendly promotion went a long way toward helping the Mets build a sizable fan base, especially as those young children matured, had children of their own, and brought them out to Shea to meet the Mets.

I fondly recall one Bordens promotion that caused quite a stir among several of my co-workers at Shea. Remember Bill ("the Judge") Gibson, Bob Mandt's assistant? That guy had a great sense of humor. Unfortunately, not everyone in the ticket department could appreciate it. Well, one day the Judge came to the back room of the ticket office and told all of the veteran union ticket guys that Bordens was so pleased with the coupon promotion that they wanted to do an inventory of which Bordens products were most popular with the fans. Was it the ice cream? If so, what flavor—vanilla, chocolate, or strawberry? Or the chocolate milk? Or maybe even the cottage cheese? The Bordens executives wanted to know. So Bill told these crusty old set-in-their-way union guys to separate all the coupons and sort them into the various product categories.

This request didn't sit very well with the guys. They really didn't want to sit there and sort through those messy and somewhat sticky coupons that had been thrown together into a large barrel and been left to sit in the hot summer sun for who knows how long! Suddenly, Frank McGuiness, who had been with the old New York Giants' baseball team and was the union representative at the time, picked up the phone and threatened to call the union with a complaint. He was livid. If Bob Mandt had not been in the office to convince Frank that it was only a joke perpetrated on them by Bill, there would have been a wildcat strike that day at Shea. And all over Bordens coupons.

The Judge once tried to pull a prank on Bob and me. Shea Stadium was originally built with the intention of someday putting a dome on it. But when Mayor Lindsay was elected, he turned down the dome project, allegedly for financial reasons. All the newspapers carried the story the day of Lindsay's decision. However, Bob and I had been out late the night before at the World's Fair and had not yet read the papers. When we arrived at the office that morning, we were greeted by a panic-stricken Bill Gibson lamenting that the guys from New York City were here to deliver a large dome and there was nobody around to sign for it! It just never stopped with Bill. He always tried to bring a bit of humor into everyone's life. That is why everybody in the National League who knew the Judge, loved him.

Mets executive Bob Mandt (*center back*, wearing glasses) hired me in 1964 as a ticket agent. He was joined in 2005 at his retirement party by his wife Norma as well as by, *left to right*, photographer Dick Collins, broadcaster Ralph Kiner, and original Met Ed Kranepool.

In 1967, Bordens initiated their "Most Popular Met" promotion. Although it turned out to be one of the more successful promotions for Bordens and the Mets, the fans found it difficult to decide which Met was most popular. Many of the players were well liked, and some even had their own fan clubs. It was also around this time that Herb Heft left the Mets to join his brother with the old Baltimore Bullets in the National Basketball Association. Herb was replaced by Arthur Richman, who had been a noted columnist for the old *Daily Mirror,* a newspaper that had folded a few years earlier. When Arthur joined the Mets, he became my boss, and, I might add, my dear friend.

Arthur and I worked together on the Most Popular Met promotion. We didn't know who at Bordens came up with this gem of an idea, and it really didn't matter. Arthur and I were determined to do our best to make it a successful promotion despite one small problem: the winning ballplayer was going to get a real live cow. What were those guys at Bordens thinking? What would a baseball player do with a cow? The contest that inaugural year turned out to be a tie between Cleon Jones and Tom Seaver. Jones backed out, saying he didn't know what to do with the damn cow, and Seaver just wanted us to donate it to someone … anyone! Leave it to Tom. His suggestion worked out perfectly. With the help of one of our New Jersey sportswriters, Bill Quinn, the cow was donated to a Boys Town in Kearney, New Jersey. It was handed over to the boys at Shea Stadium before a game, and publicity pictures of the boys, the players, and, of course, the cow were taken by the press. Thanks to Tom's creative suggestion and Arthur's contacts with the media, it worked out fine.

We also worked with the Long Island Railroad for a few years on a promotion called the "Hot Stove Express." The railroad arranged for us to use a couple of their trains to visit various Long Island towns with our players and participating sponsors. They assured that a particular route would be closed for our use on a designated Saturday morning, and we would bring our group to the local high school gym or athletic field, where the players would meet the fans. The theme usually went something like, "You came out to Shea and supported us during the season; now it's our turn to come and visit you." The Long Island Railroad loved this promotion because it was great public relations. Bordens would give out free samples of their products. And Rheingold would distribute baseball schedules of the upcoming season and brochures with their names and promotion on them.

Thanks to our many sponsors—which included not only Rheingold Beer, Bordens, and the Long Island Railroad but also Manufacturer's Hanover Trust Company and the old Howard Clothes Corporation—all of us in the Mets' front office kept busy during the off-season, promoting our loveable Mets to their adoring public. As Chairman of the Board M. Donald Grant used to say, our sponsors were valued members of our Mets family.

Chapter Ten
Recalling Some
Special Moments

The original public address announcer for the New York Mets was a gentleman by the name of Jack Lee. Jack started with the organization in the old Polo Grounds in 1962. One day in 1966, Jack advised Jim Thomson that he had been offered a great opportunity to be the official race caller at Yonkers and Roosevelt raceways. Roosevelt Raceway is now closed. But in those days, calling the races at both tracks would be a full-time position for Jack and would therefore conflict with his part-time summer work for the Mets. Once the Mets knew Jack was leaving, they had to find a replacement quickly. During the search, I was asked to fill in as the PA announcer. So Mr. Met actually called a few games at Shea in 1966.

The three of us who worked in the control room together—Jack, our beloved organist Jane Jarvis, and myself—became fast friends. After Jack left, and while the team was on the road, I had the opportunity to practice in the afternoon with the live mike over the PA system. It sounded OK to Jim and Arthur, and my debut was all set. I really enjoyed announcing, young ham that I was, and looked forward to each game. It did get a little confusing at times when there were lineup changes in the middle of the game. But it all worked out fine.

There was one incident I will never forget during my three short weeks as PA announcer at Shea Stadium. I received a call from the Jets' PA announcer one day. He asked if I could fill in for him one Sunday afternoon. I told him I had never done a football game. Nonetheless, he was very encouraging and told me he could arrange to have someone up at the booth with me to act as a spotter, since doing football requires announcing every play. I accepted the challenge and agreed to help out.

The spotter assigned to me was an old friend of Bob Mandt's and mine from St. John's University. His name was Bernie Beglane, and what a help he was for me that day! Prior to the game, I made a telephone call to the man who had been my speech teacher at John Adams High School in Queens, Bob Shepherd. Does that name sound familiar? Well it should. Bob is the PA announcer for both the New York Yankees and the Football Giants. To this day, his famous voice can be heard echoing through the canyons of Yankee Stadium, as well as Giants Stadium in New Jersey. In fact, it was Bob who nominated me for the Dramatics Award I received on graduating from high school. Luckily, we had kept in touch all those years.

Several days before my debut for the Jets at Shea Stadium, I spent over an hour on the phone with Bob, picking his brains and seeking advice. The most important thing he taught me about football was to maintain complete focus on what was happening on the field. Unlike the leisurely pace of baseball, where you simply announce the next batter, in football you have to be on top of every play.

Thanks to a couple of old St. John's guys, Bernie Beglane and Bob Shepherd, my football debut went well, except for one very obvious and embarrassing blunder in the first quarter. I guess PA announcers need to warm up too, because on the first completed pass of the game for the Jets, I belted out enthusiastically, "Maynard's pass to Namath was complete!" The names, of course, should have been reversed. Joe Namath, after all, was one of the greatest quarterbacks of all time, and Don Maynard was an All-Pro receiver and future Hall of Famer. What was I thinking? I hoped that since it was only the first quarter of the game, it might have gone unnoticed by the fans. No way! When I arrived at Breslin's restaurant after the game, boy, did I hear it from all my friends!

I got to know onetime Dodger pitcher Ralph Branca, *left,* when he came to Shea for old-timer games. Ralph's son-in-law is Bobby Valentine, former manager of the Mets.

My three-week stint as PA announcer ended when the Mets hired the great radio sportscaster Jack Lightcap as our permanent announcer at Shea. Jack was not only a great announcer, but he also fit in well with our mischievous crew in the control booth. For example, one day after a game in which the Mets won, Jack, myself, and the rest of the guys were happily singing along as Jane played the organ, not realizing that the stadium PA microphone was still on. Our off-key voices resonated so loudly over the Shea's PA system that it drowned out Bob Murphy's postgame recap on TV! How that lovely Jane Jarvis managed to perform on the organ with such class and professionalism while putting up with the rest of us in the control booth was a miracle.

Shea Stadium belonged to the City of New York and the Mets were the primary tenants. Therefore, when the team was out of town, the city would sometimes schedule other events, such as a middleweight prize fight. I will never forget a marathon rock concert at Shea featuring Janis Joplin. That was when I first met and became friends with the union stagehands from IATSE Local No. 4. They arrived at Shea a few days before the concert to set up the stage and work on the sound system. What a great bunch of guys they were. And what a great concert! It lasted for hours. Everyone enjoyed the evening ... well, everyone except one person.

Johnny McCarthy was the Mets' head groundskeeper. And what a job he had ahead of him. Between the fans running onto the field during the concert and the performers walking to and from the stage, the field needed a lot of work to get it back into shape for baseball. And John only had a few days to work his miracle before the Mets returned to Shea from their road trip. Such problems are now a thing of the past, since the Mets' lease today precludes holding non-baseball events at the stadium during the baseball season. But back then, Johnny McCarthy and several of his key crew members—including Pete Flynn, the current head groundskeeper for the Mets, and Joe Costello—had to work their butts off to get that field into pristine shape. And amazingly, they always succeeded.

Of course, the most famous concert ever held at Shea Stadium had to be the 1964 Beatles concert. I am embarrassed to admit that at the time I had no idea how big that event was going to be. One evening, during one of our ballgames, an usher asked me if I could get him tickets for the upcoming Beatles concert. I didn't have the slightest idea what he was talking about. Who, or what, were the Beatles? Not wanting to show my ignorance, I told him I would find out and get back to him. I went immediately to Bob Mandt's office and asked, "Who the hell are the Beatles, and what do we have to do with them?" No sooner had the words left my mouth than Bob pointed to a man sitting in his office whom I had never met before and said, "Dan, I'd like you to meet Sid Bernstein. Sid's promoting the concert with the

Beatles." Talk about embarrassing moments. Thankfully, Sid was a great guy, and we all shared a good laugh.

Several weeks later, a group of us from the ticket department and front office were called into Jim Thomson's office for a meeting with Sid Bernstein and Bob Mandt. They told us that they needed several of us to walk around the stadium during the Beatles' concert to observe the crowd and make sure no one filmed the concert with professional equipment. Naturally, Sid had secured all filming rights and didn't want anyone stealing that asset. In those days, it really wasn't very difficult to spot professional cameras. They were bulky and obtrusive, nothing like today's miniaturized equipment. We had been selected for this assignment because of our detailed knowledge of the ballpark. And, of course, most of us agreed to work for that eventful night.

Frank Cashen, *center*, was executive vice president of the Baltimore Orioles when the Mets beat them in the 1969 World Series. He joined the Mets in 1980 and reorganized the team, setting the stage for the Mets' second World Series championship in 1986. He is shown here with Tug McGraw and Bob Murphy.

On the evening of that historic event, reality had finally set in, and I realized how memorable the night was going to be. We all assembled downstairs in the runway behind home plate to get our location assignments. Just a few feet away in the umpires' room, the Beatles were dressing and preparing for the evening's performance. Finally they emerged from their dressing room. Even I started to feel the excitement in the air, and I wasn't even a fan! As the Fab Four walked by, I got up my nerve and like a little kid blurted out unabashedly, "Break a leg, guys!" Not being a fan of theirs at the time, I didn't know any of their names. But one of them, either Paul McCartney or John Lennon, did reply rather matter-of-factly, "Thank you, mate." In later years, I would tell my family and friends, "Not only did I see the Beatles perform at Shea Stadium, I also got paid for it!" How many people can say that?

One of the more popular events in baseball occurs in the off-season, in January just before spring training. It's the annual New York Baseball Writers' Dinner. The event is like a pre-season baseball convention because all of the teams in both leagues are represented. This is also the night when the Most Valuable Player, Rookie of the Year, and Cy Young awards and other special honors are presented. Jack Lang, formerly of the *Long Island Press* and *New York Daily News*, coordinates this prestigious affair each year and, together with his staff of fellow writers, always does such a great job. Guests, including former ballplayers, politicians and celebrities, come from all over the country to talk baseball and honor the achievements of the previous season.

Because they are the local teams, both the Mets and Yankees usually host their own pre-dinner cocktail parties for all the invited guests. There was one such party I will never forget. It was the Mets' black-tie affair at the old Toots Shor's Restaurant. I was in an impassioned discussion with Bill (the Judge) Gibson about some trade the Mets had just made, when someone tapped me on the shoulder from behind. Without looking back and seeing who it was first, I said, matter-of-factly, "I'll be right with you." Finally I turned around and saw Bowie Kuhn, the Commissioner of Baseball, and standing right next to him was New York Governor Nelson Rockefeller. Here was the

Commissioner of Baseball trying to introduce me to the Governor of New York, and all I had to say was, "I'll be right with you"! It all happened so fast that I hoped the commissioner hadn't noticed my remark. No such luck. I really heard it from my co-workers next day!

I made yet another faux pas I would like to forget. Whenever there was a special day or promotion at Shea, Arthur Richman and I would divide the various assignments between us. This particular event was a season opener against the San Francisco Giants, and the great Hall of Famer Juan Marichal was scheduled to pitch against the Mets. Willie Mays, Willie McCovey, Orlando Cepeda, and Juan Marichal naturally had all played at Shea Stadium previously, but never on Opening Day. So this season opener was very special, and a sellout crowd was expected.

While Arthur took some dignitaries upstairs to the owner's room, he asked me to officially greet the mayor, who at the time was John Lindsay. Mr. Lindsay was a very charming, distinguished, and outgoing guy. I thought he might like to mingle with some of the citizens of our fair town, so I escorted him and his entourage upstairs to the press level at Shea, walked them through the Diamond Club where season ticket holders usually gathered both before and after the games, and then escorted them on the owner's room.

We went through the Diamond Club so fast that hardly anyone recognized the mayor. When we arrived at the owner's room, one of his aides thanked me and asked me my name. I responded cordially and asked for his. I thought I had made a friend in the mayor's office. No such luck. It seems that Mayor Lindsay was not as gregarious as I had thought. He wanted to go up to the press level via the back way and did not want any contact with the fans. In hindsight, I should have taken him up via the press elevator instead, which would have avoided all the fans. It's just that I recalled hearing about mayors like Jimmy Walker and Fiorello LaGuardia, who enjoyed mingling with the people, and I thought Mayor Lindsay was cut from the same cloth. Well, I guess I was wrong. Jim Thomson told me the next day that he had heard from M. Donald Grant, our chairman of the board, that Mr. Lindsay was somewhat annoyed about the incident. However, if it was any consolation, Jim confided that he would have done the very same thing.

I grew up as a Brooklyn Dodgers fan, and Gil Hodges was my favorite ballplayer. So when Gil joined the Mets as manager in 1967, no one was more thrilled than me. One of the coaches Gil brought along with him was Eddie Yost. When I was a youngster growing up in Richmond Hill, Queens, in New York, Eddie was the star third baseman for the old Washington Senators. As their leadoff hitter, he was known as "the walking man" because of his keen eye at the plate and his ability to get on base. Eddie was another one of my boyhood baseball heroes. And whenever the Senators would come into town to play the Yankees, a bunch of us would find out which Mass Eddie would be attending on Sunday and go down to the church to greet him. How many people can say that they actually worked with two of their boyhood heroes? I really was living a charmed life!

My former neighbor, actor Matthew Broderick, is a huge Mets fan. We have been to a couple of games together and he even rode on the New York Waterway Shea Express with me. Fans on the boat were thrilled to chat with this popular star.

I have previously mentioned M. Donald Grant, chairman of the Mets' board and chief advisor to the principal owner, Mrs. Joan Payson. Mr. Grant was constantly in touch with both Bob Mandt and Jim Thomson regarding the operation of the ball club. On a more personal level, one of his favorite duties was attending our annual Christmas party and distributing gifts to all of the employees. He loved to play Santa Claus at these affairs, but never wore the costume or beard. Because of his limited contact with the employees, Mr. Grant never really knew their names or positions in the organization, so each year someone had to help him sort this all out. That someone was usually me. The gifts were always arranged by department and employee name. When the time came to begin handing out the presents, I would pick up each one, hand it to Mr. Grant, and whisper to him the name and department of each employee. He wanted so badly to convince us all that he really knew each of us personally. Of course we knew otherwise. But it was the thought and effort that counted. The annual Christmas party was the social highlight of our year, and the gifts were always big league. Mr. Grant would always use the expression the "Mets family," and looking back, I now realize how right he really was.

Chapter Eleven
That Championship Season

The 1968 season under Gil Hodges turned out to be the Mets' most successful to date. The team not only had a then-record high of seventy-three victories, but for the first time they also finished ahead of their expansion rivals, the Houston Astros (formerly the Houston Colt .45's). Several new faces appeared at Shea in 1968 and early 1969, thanks to some trades by Bing Devine and player recommendations by Gil Hodges. Bing was to leave the organization in 1968 to return to St. Louis. But before leaving, he made a key trade with the Chicago White Sox that brought center fielder Tommy Agee and infielder Al Weis to the Mets. Both would play pivotal roles in the team's 1969 championship season. Since Gil had managed the American League Washington Senators in 1967, he knew both players very well. He really liked Agee's speed, power, and defensive skills in center field, and Al Weis was a perfect backup for our infield of Bud Harrelson at shortstop and Ken Boswell at second base.

Another piece of the puzzle was completed when veteran Ed Charles came over from the Kansas City Athletics in 1967 to play third base. By the time Ed joined the team, the Mets had had over thirty different third basemen in their brief history. He was a real team guy and clutch professional on the field, and he was a great help to me with the Speakers Bureau Program off the field as well. Ed loved to talk to the young fans, which I understand he still does to this day, and is very heavily involved with youth work.

Onetime Mets' star outfielder Ron Swoboda and his wife Cecilia are former neighbors and good friends. They now live in New Orleans, where Ron broadcasts games for the Mets' triple-A affiliate, the Zephyrs, and Cecilia is a teacher.

The Mets began to show significant improvement on the field during the summer of 1968. But as soon as the 1968 baseball season was over, our cotenants at Shea Stadium and good friends, the New York Jets, began making some history of their own and soon became the talk of the town. They won the championship of the American Football League and went on to upset the NFL's best, the Baltimore Colts, in Super Bowl III. In fact, they were the first AFL team to beat the NFL Champions in a Super Bowl and debunked the myth that the AFL could not play with the NFL. It was this single and decisive victory by Joe "Willie" Namath and company that ultimately led to the merger of the upstart AFL with the old-guard NFL. Jets' owner Sonny Werblin and legendary coach Weeb Ewbank deserved most of the credit for building such a stellar championship football organization.

Since the Jets and the Mets grew up together, we were hoping that the winning atmosphere they brought to Shea Stadium would somehow rub off on us during the subsequent 1969 baseball season. I will never forget seeing Jets' center Sam DeLuca's Super Bowl ring for the first time. It was certainly impressive. We were all hoping that our day was drawing near, maybe not a championship season, but a winning season nonetheless. Our fans certainly deserved it.

The 1969 team had a certain character and class about it. Even the coaching staff Gil had brought with him the year before from Washington was the embodiment of class and baseball acumen. Joe Pignatano, former catcher for the Brooklyn Dodgers, was the bullpen coach. Joe was well liked and respected by all the players because of his positive attitude and knowledge of the game. He also helped me out considerably with the Speakers Bureau during the winter. Eddie Yost was Gil's third-base coach with the Senators and held the same assignment with the 1969 Mets. Eddie was a guy who really knew the game and, as a teacher during the off-season, was great with the younger players. Rube Walker was our pitching coach and was probably one of the most underrated coaches in baseball. What he did with that young staff was amazing. In fact, Rube was the man responsible for starting the five-man pitching rotation (replacing the traditional four-man rotation), a concept which today is the linchpin of every major league team's pitching strategy. The record speaks for itself. Both Tom Seaver and Nolan Ryan went on to pitch well into their forties, with both having Hall of Fame careers. Then, of course, there was Yogi Berra, who was asked to stay on as coach when Gil came aboard. Yogi took over as first-base coach, but he also proved to be invaluable as the team's hitting coach. He always seemed to be there when one of the guys needed some advice. Whenever Gil would call for early batting practice, Yogi would be right there with all the coaches, either pitching or watching behind the batting screen. As the players batted, Yogi would look for that little something that would either help a player out of a slump or get that player to achieve the next level as a hitter. Despite his reputation and demeanor, Yogi Berra has to be considered one of the greatest baseball minds ever to be associated with the game.

Gil and his coaches believed in leadership by example. Gil and Joe Pignatano would come to the ballpark early every day to go over lineups and game plans. This attitude certainly affected the players, because everyone started arriving at the park early. And if a player was in a batting slump or was just having problems with his hitting, Gil and the coaches were always there for him, regardless of the time of day. In fact, Jerry Grote, arguably the best defensive catcher in Mets history, told me how Gil took him aside one day and completely changed his batting stance. Jerry came to Mets from the Houston Astros in 1965 as a stellar defensive catcher with a so-so bat, but later he became one of the better-hitting catchers in the game.

When Bing Devine left the Mets in 1968 to go back to St. Louis, Mets' ownership decided to keep the general managership in the family and elevated Johnny Murphy from assistant general manager to general manager. This was a perfect choice, because John and Gil got along so well and agreed on the direction they wanted the young club to take. Gil and John agreed, for example, that adding a few veteran pitchers would help anchor the young pitching staff in 1969, so John went out and got Don Cardwell as a starter and Ron Taylor as a reliever.

While the Mets were preparing for their 1969 season, Whitey Herzog, one of Bing Devine's imports from the St. Louis Cardinals organization, was running the Mets' farm system. Whitey was a baseball man's baseball man. He had a great knowledge of the game and a keen eye for young talent. It was Whitey who recommended another young pitching prospect to the Mets organization, Gary Gentry. Gary made the big club in 1969 and joined Tom Seaver, Jerry Koosman, and Nolan Ryan in what was then a very young, yet formidable starting rotation.

Nolan Ryan was unpredictable during his rookie year in 1969. Some days he was unhittable, throwing nothing but fastballs past the hitters. On other days, he couldn't have found the plate with a cannon. He was the team's fourth starter and at times was banished to the bullpen to work out his wildness. Nonetheless, Nolan was the talk of the National League, with that awesome fastball that approached one hundred miles per hour. He was a very quiet and polite young man from Alvin, Texas, who never really felt comfortable in New York City. He made a few appearances for our Speakers Bureau Program but preferred to spend more time with his family. His lovely wife, Ruth, was a great tennis player and, from what I had heard, had the talent to turn professional. Obviously, they both focused on Nolan's baseball career, for which I guess we should all be grateful. The Hall of Fame is most certainly waiting for Nolan Ryan.

The Hall of Fame has already welcomed the young anchor of that '69 Mets' pitching staff and one of my favorite Mets of all time, Tom Seaver. It was not only Tom's greatness on the mound but also his leadership and example off the field that made him so remarkable. When he first joined the organization, I knew he was different from the other players. Tom was genuinely interested in the type of work Arthur Richman and I were doing with the various promotions. He wanted to learn as much as he could about his new organization off the field, and that was refreshing. Tom Seaver is also a class guy. As I stated earlier, my old friend Jim Fitzgerald from the World's Fair was also a Naval Recruitment Officer and had heard that Tom had been in the Marine Corps Reserve while at USC. Jim asked me if Tom would visit St. Albans Naval Hospital and see some of the patients, most of whom had been injured in Vietnam. The war, at that time, was escalating and seriously dividing the country. I had no idea of what Tom's view was on the war and was somewhat reluctant to ask, since the entire nation was so divided on this issue. Without hesitation, Tom told me to schedule the date. We selected an afternoon when the team had a night game and Tom was not pitching. The visit included just Jim Fitzgerald, Tom Seaver, and me. As usual, we asked for no publicity, but St. Albans wanted to cover the visit for their own publications. As for us, however, this visit was strictly between Tom and the patients. While making the rounds at the hospital, a surgeon asked me if Tom could visit one of the patients in the orthopedic unit. He told me that this young man was the son of a former Brooklyn Dodgers pitcher and one of the original Mets, Clem Labine. Naturally, we went right over and visited with the young man. He had been badly injured in Vietnam, and his spirits were somewhat down. Nonetheless, Tom was great with him and was able to get the young man to crack a smile or two before we left. I saw Clem later that year at an old-timers' affair. He told me that his son was doing fine and really got a boost from our visit.

Gil Hodges, our manager that year, also heard about the visit and thanked me personally. Gil had been teammates with Clem Labine, on both the Brooklyn Dodgers and New York Mets, and always appreciated a good deed.

Tom Seaver and Gary Gentry were two of the star pitchers on the 1969 team. Seaver won twenty games and Gentry twelve. The "miracle Mets" shocked America by posting their first winning season ever and capturing the World Series title.

The 1969 season started off uneventfully. The organization knew it had an exciting, young, and competitive team. But no one was thinking of a World Series championship. The Mets' record had been so abysmal that no one thought they could go from being the worst team in the league in 1962 to the best in 1969. Looking back, we should have known better.

1969 was an expansion year for the National League, with the Montreal Expos coming to the Eastern Division and the San Diego Padres coming on board in the Western Division. This was also the first year of divisional play. Despite playing the fledgling Montreal Expos for their season opener, the Mets lost that game 11 to 10, an inauspicious beginning if ever there was one. The team went on to play uninspired baseball early on in the campaign. Finally, after about a month into the season, the Mets reached the coveted .500 mark with an 18-18 record. Normally, this would be a cause for celebration, since the Mets had never reached .500 that late in the season. However, this was a different Mets team with a different attitude. And when asked about how it felt to be playing .500 baseball in May, it was Tom Seaver who wondered aloud what the big deal was all about. This same feeling carried through the clubhouse and even to those of us in the front office. We knew we had an improved team, maybe not a contender, but definitely a young, scrappy, and improved baseball team.

The Chicago Cubs, led by their colorful manager Leo Durocher, were tabbed by the pre-season experts as the team to beat. As late as July 16, the Mets were in second place in the National League East, three and one half games behind the Cubs. This was an amazing feat in and of itself, given the historically poor record of the franchise.

The magic began on the fateful evening of July 9. Tom Seaver was on the mound at Shea Stadium against the Cubs' great lefthander Ken Holtzman. It was a sellout crowd, and Tom "Terrific" put on a show. He retired the first twenty-four Cubs he faced, for a perfect eight innings, giving up only a clean single to weak-hitting Cubs outfielder Jimmy Qualls leading off the ninth. The crowd went wild and gave Tom a standing ovation that lasted about ten minutes. It was only July, and the team still had a long way to go, but you began to sense something exciting was about to happen.

On July 20, Apollo 11 commanded by Neil Armstrong landed on the Moon. For the first time in history, mankind looked up at the moon glistening in the heavens, knowing that several of our own were there looking down at us. It was a strange yet exhilarating feeling for all of us, a miracle of science and a testament to man's desire to explore and seek the truth. And if the old adage were true about putting a man on the moon before the Mets won the World Series, the moon landing opened the way for the Mets to win a championship in the Age of Aquarius.

At the All-Star break, general manager Johnny Murphy rewarded several of us in the front office with a trip to the midsummer classic in Washington, DC. The 1969 All-Star break was a great experience for me, one I will never forget. Because 1969 was the celebration of baseball's centennial, a big banquet was held to commemorate this milestone. All of baseball's elite attended. And thanks to John, I was there.

When the regular season resumed, the team started to play inspired baseball and, incredibly, kept inching closer and closer to the Chicago Cubs in the standings. Finally, on September 9, the team defeated the Cubs 3 to 2 at Shea Stadium and took over first place in the Eastern Division of the National League. The Mets never let go of first place that year and won their division by eight games. There were different heroes every day who contributed to the team's victories, players like Al Weis, who hit a couple of dramatic home runs in Chicago, and Gary Gentry, who pitched great games against San Francisco and Chicago. The Mets also had the great fortune of having two reliable backup catchers for Jerry Grote: Duffy Dyer and veteran J. C. Martin, whom the Mets acquired from the Chicago White Sox. There was young Wayne Garrett, who played third base behind the veteran Ed "the Glider" Charles. Ken Boswell was the regular second baseman, with Al Weis backing up both Boswell at second and Harrelson at shortstop. Slugger Donn Clendenon, acquired by the Mets from the Pittsburgh Pirates during the season, played first base, with Art Shamsky alternating between first base and right field. Art had joined the team from the Cincinnati Reds the year before. Cleon Jones, Tommy Agee, and Ron Swoboda completed the outfield, left to right.

The Atlanta Braves were the Western Division Champions in 1969 and faced the Mets in the first-ever National League Championship Series, a best-of-five series. Many Met fans were content to have won their division and thought the Mets had no chance whatsoever of beating the heavily favored, hard-hitting Braves, led by home-run king, Hank Aaron. And in fact, the Mets were really up against it, because they had to play the first two games in Atlanta and face the great knuckleballer Phil Niekro in Game One. The Mets not only defeated Niekro and the Braves in the first game, they also went on to sweep all three games against the Braves, with the final victory coming at Shea Stadium on October 6. In that game, Nolan Ryan came in to relieve Gary Gentry and struck out seven Braves in seven innings. But the Mets' work wasn't over yet. If this was going to be the first-ever championship season for the New York Mets, there was still the American League champion to contend with.

Over in the American League, the Baltimore Orioles and Minnesota Twins were battling it out for the pennant. Lou Niss, the Mets' traveling secretary, had to make hotel arrangements to cover the team for both cities. As it turned out, Baltimore won, and once again, the experts were saying that the Mets were in over their heads. The team could never beat Baltimore. After all, the Orioles had power, speed, great defense, and even greater pitching, with four twenty-game winners on its staff. But in 1969, the Mets seemed to have an even greater force on their side.

After the Mets beat the Cubs on September 8, I turned to Johnny Murphy in the press box and said, incredulously, "God is alive and living at Shea Stadium." Everything seemed to be going our way, all the breaks, all the calls, everything. It was almost as if the Mets were a team of destiny. John loved my comment and repeated it to a few people, including, I suspect, Tom Seaver. In between games of a doubleheader that day, I went downstairs to the clubhouse for a break. There was Tom, sitting all by himself after winning the first game. Before the press approached him for his thoughts on the game, I went over to Tom and congratulated him on his fine pitching performance. The next day, I picked up the morning paper and saw the headline, "Tom Seaver—God is Alive and Living at Shea Stadium." He probably did say it, and it did sound better coming from him, but I just want to go on record that I said it first.

The first two games of the 1969 World Series were played at Baltimore's Memorial Stadium. Arthur Richman and I were to prepare all the pregame and special event activities for the series when the team returned to Shea Stadium for Games Three, Four and Five. There would be the usual Armed Forces Color Guard and military bands, which were arranged by our military contact, Jim Fitzgerald. Arthur and I also had to secure someone to sing the National Anthem for each game, as well as celebrities to throw out the first ball. That honor usually went to the mayor, the governor, or some celebrity who happened to be in town. We finished the Atlanta series on Sunday and spent all day Monday having meetings with Jim Thomson, public relations director Harold Weisman, and his assistant Matt Winnick. We had a prominent Broadway star scheduled to sing the anthem for Game Four, Gordon MacRae, who starred in such classic musicals as *Oklahoma!* and *Carousel,* and for Game Five we were lucky to have Pearl Bailey available to sing.

After all the arrangements were finalized, Arthur and Harold went off to Baltimore and joined the rest of our official party for the first two games of the World Series. That left me to take care of any last-minute problems on the home front. What problems could possibly arise at the last minute, I asked myself. Answer: the biggest problem of all, ticket requests. It seems that each department in the organization was given an allotment of World Series tickets for the games in Baltimore. These were for our sponsors and people whom we had worked with throughout the year. Arthur left me in charge of these tickets, but most of our people were taken care of; at least, that's what I had been told.

While the Mets were getting set to start the series in Baltimore, there had to be at least twenty people waiting for me to buy World Series tickets for Games One and Two. These were people we knew and who just took it upon themselves to stop by, assuming that we had tickets for them. Arthur heard about this and called me from Baltimore. The problem was taken care of by Bob Mandt, who was able to secure some extra tickets, probably from the allotment set aside by the Orioles. So now I had extra tickets and started contacting my friends in the airlines to see if anyone wanted to travel down to Baltimore to cheer on the Mets. I don't think Baltimore ever did sell out their first two games of the 1969 World Series. Perhaps their fans, too, thought the World Series was a lock for the Birds and that the Mets didn't deserve to be on the same field as their beloved Orioles.

The 1969 World Series began on a sour note for the Mets; the Orioles beat Tom Seaver 4 to 1. But despite Baltimore beating the ace of New York's staff, the Mets' morale did not sink. Instead, the guys came right back to win Game Two behind the brilliant pitching of Jerry Koosman, who pitched six innings of no-hit baseball. With late-inning relief help from Ron Taylor, the Mets went on to beat the Orioles 2 to 1. We were going back to New York with the series tied at one game apiece.

With the Mets back at Shea Stadium for the next three games, my responsibilities seemed to never end. Helping me for Games Three to Five was a guy by the name of Walter Carberry. Walter helped us coordinate all the pregame activities. When I escorted the band onto the field or went out to meet the Color Guard or the person throwing out the first ball, Walter was the man who would keep everything under control. The pregame activities during the '69 World Series would never have gone as smoothly as they did if it hadn't been for Walter and a few others, namely the guys at the executive entrance and the press gate. Everyone who arrived at these locations expected special attention, and the guys manning those key entrances were experts at making the fans feel special. Believe it or not, there is an art to this, and these experienced guys were invaluable.

Another major part of all this excitement was the attitude of the Mets players and coaches. They were so loose and enjoying the experience so much that they approached the World Series as if the games were simply part of the regular season. After all, the Mets were huge underdogs. The team's cooperation with the press and others made a positive impression on everyone. For example, during batting practice before Game Three, one of the VIPs I was to escort up to the owner's room was former U.S. Postmaster General James J. Farley. Mr. Farley, who had served under Franklin Roosevelt, was then in his eighties. He was known as a great baseball fan; his favorite team was the Yankees in the days of Babe Ruth and Lou Gehrig. M. Donald Grant phoned us from the owner's room and said Mr. Farley hadn't arrived, so we checked downstairs. Sure enough, his tickets had been picked up and he had been directed to the owner's room, but no one knew exactly where he and his party were. So I decided to look outside on the field, where batting practice was in progress, and sure enough, sitting by himself alongside the Met dugout in the owner's box, was Mr. Farley. He was wearing one of those summer straw hats like you saw in the twenties and thirties, thoroughly absorbed in the Mets as they took batting practice. When I approached Mr. Farley and advised him that he was expected upstairs, he asked me to wait a few minutes, because he was enjoying batting practice so much. He commented on how young the players were and what a great time they appeared to be having. It was obvious to all that this team had nothing to lose.

The enthusiasm and excitement continued into Game Three when Gary Gentry, with some great relief help from Nolan Ryan, shut out the Orioles by a score of 5 to 0. That was the game Tommy Agree made two of the greatest outfield catches ever in World Series history. The Mets were playing like a team of destiny, while the heavily favored Orioles appeared to be tight and somewhat perplexed by the position in which they had found themselves.

Even with all of the festivities and excitement surrounding the 1969 World Series, it was impossible to forget that the war in Vietnam was still going strong. Mayor Lindsay declared October 16, 1969, to be "Moratorium Day" throughout the city as a protest against the war. He ordered all city buildings to fly their flags at half-mast as a sign of protest. This moratorium was not recognized by either the federal government or, naturally, the armed forces. In fact, many in the armed services took offense at Mayor Lindsay's position. As a result, Jim Fitzgerald advised us that neither the Armed Forces Band nor the Color Guard would participate in the pregame ceremonies for Game Four of the World Series. We had built some temporary bleachers out in center field to accommodate disabled veterans from the nearby veterans' hospitals, but unfortunately this part of the ceremony also had to be cancelled. Thanks to Mayor Lindsay, there was no band or Color Guard for Game Four of the 1969 World Series.

Thankfully, we still had the National Anthem singer on board with us, Gordon MacRae. It was my assignment that day to meet Gordon and bring him upstairs to the owner's room and then down to the field for the National Anthem. I also had to let him know that he would begin that day without any musical accompaniment. I was so nervous about having to tell Gordon that. I truly did not know how he would react.

When Gordon and his agent arrived, I knew my worries were over. He was a regular guy who made me feel like an old friend. As we made our way upstairs, I broke the bad news to him. However, Gordon seemed to be genuinely unfazed by it all. He shrugged his shoulders and said it wasn't the first time this had happened to him and it wouldn't be the last. His only concern at that moment was for his young daughter. She was opening that night in the Broadway musical *Hair*. There was a nude scene in the show, and he was concerned about how his wife, actress Sheila MacRae, was going to react to her daughter appearing in that scene. What a trooper!

As it turned out, the pregame festivities for Game Four went perfectly. The master showman that he was, Gordon asked the crowd to sing along with him, which they did, loud and strong. Because of public outcry, the mayor's moratorium had been lifted some days before, but by then it was too late to make arrangements to secure the services of the Armed Forces Band in time for Game Four. Thankfully, however, we were able to get the veterans to the game.

Tom Seaver took the mound in Game Four and beat Mike Cuellar 2 to 1 in ten innings. The Mets were now up three games to one, with one more game to play at Shea Stadium. For the first time, I began to sense an air of confidence among some of the Mets players. This brashness was best exemplified during batting practice just before Game Five. Lou Niss, the team's traveling secretary, announced that, in the event of a loss that day, all bags must be outside the players lounge one hour after the game, so that they could be put aboard the bus for the trip back to Baltimore. Lou was just doing his job, since every detail had to be worked out, win or lose. After Lou made this announcement, Buddy Harrelson, another one of our quiet leaders, whispered to me so no one could hear, "I'm not packing my bags, because we're not going back to Baltimore." Bud said this very seriously, and when I mentioned it to him years later, he was surprised I remembered. Little did Bud realize that if that statement had gotten into the papers and the Mets had lost Game Five, the team would have been in big trouble.

The pregame ceremonies for Game Five were all finalized. The Armed Forces Band and Color Guard were ready to perform. And once again I was assigned to coordinate all the specifics to ensure that the National Anthem went off without a hitch. Singing the anthem that day was the great entertainer and singer, Pearl Bailey. Her appearance was a real coup for the Mets organization. Pearl was the "Queen of Broadway," performing in the popular musical *Hello, Dolly!* The play, which had featured Carol Channing and others in the lead role, had closed after a number of very successful years. In the late 1960s, the producers reopened the musical with an African-American ensemble. They cast Pearl in the title role. The revival was an instant success, and the show once again became the hottest ticket in town.

Pearl was a big Mets fan and attended several games during the season with Joan Hodges, manager Gil Hodges' wife. When Pearl was asked to sing the National Anthem before Game Five, she was sincerely moved. I met Pearl at the executive entrance the morning of Game Five. She was running a little late, so we did not go upstairs to meet with the owners. Instead, we went directly outside to the runway that leads to the home plate area. Just as we reached the playing field, Jerry Koosman, the Mets' starting pitcher, was returning from the bullpen after taking his warmup pitches. I introduced Jerry to Pearl, who immediately invited all the Mets to see *Hello, Dolly!* after the series. Incredulously, Jerry got extremely excited about the invitation and wanted to make sure the wives were invited as well. Here is the guy who, in just a few minutes, would be trying to pitch the Mets to their first World Series championship before millions of people, and all he was concerned about was his wife seeing *Hello Dolly!* Talk about being relaxed!

Even though the Orioles got off to a 2 to 0 lead in Game Five, Al Weis and Donn Clendenon both homered, giving the Mets a 5 to 3 victory and the first World Championship in the franchise's history. When Cleon Jones squeezed that fly ball off the bat of future Mets' manager Davey Johnson for the final out of the series, all hell broke loose in New York. It was one of those moments in life you simply never forget.

I was up in the press box when the last out was made. PA announcer Jack Lightcap, organist Jane Jarvis, the electricians in the booth, and I broke out the champagne to celebrate this incredible achievement. A short while later, I called Bob Mandt in the ticket office, and we all decided to join the players in the clubhouse. On the way down, I ran into our general manager John Murphy. I remember congratulating him and seeing how calm he was about the whole thing. It was amazing how much alike he and Gil Hodges were. They were certainly happy and proud for the organization and the city of New York. But they also realized that this was the players' celebration. Johnny and Gil put the pieces together, but the players had to execute. Being former major league players themselves, Johnny Murphy and Gil Hodges understood better than most what the players themselves were feeling at this most euphoric time of their careers. When Bob Mandt and I arrived in the Mets' clubhouse, naturally the place was in chaos. I went over to Gil Hodges, who was standing next to Johnny Murphy, and congratulated him. Gil graciously accepted my congratulations and said something to me which I will never forget. He wanted to let me know how much he appreciated all my hard work and the personal sacrifices I had made for the organization, sometimes over and above the call of duty. Gil, his players, and the coaches always praised our front office as being the best in baseball. He wanted me and the rest of the crew to know that we all had a part in this miraculous achievement.

My brother Bob kept this scorecard of the fifth and final game of the 1969 World Series. Note the upper right, where he wrote, "Bunt single while I was getting hot dogs and hot chocolate."

Celebrations after the World Series' victory, a ticker-tape parade down Broadway's Canyon of Champions, the love of fans for a team that came out of nowhere to achieve greatness ... these were once-in-a-lifetime experiences that I will never forget. I was working with the classiest group of people you will ever meet, but I was only a small part of the day-in, day-out operations. Nothing glamorous. But isn't that how life is for most of us? Nothing glamorous. We all can't be major league ballplayers, famous movie stars, or high-profile rock artists. Instead, we get up each morning, go to work, and try to do the best job we possibly can, both for our own sake and for the sake of our families and everyone in the organization. As Gil used to say, to win—for an organization to achieve its goals—each one in the organization has a job to do and challenges to face. And for Gil and the rest of the organization during those early years, the New York Mets took on their challenges one at a time and won. I'm just grateful that in my own small and humble way I was able to help the Mets achieve our little miracle.

978-0-595-46260-5
0-595-46260-X